# POWER DRILLS

## FOR TEAM TENNIS

*Renata Marcinkowska*

**Renata Marcinkowska**

**SUMMERTOWN**
*Signal Mountain, Tennessee*

Copyright © The Summertown Company, Inc.

Published by Summertown Texts
P. O. Box 453
Signal Mountain, TN 37377-0453
1 (800) 742-5710
e-mail: rivrol@fmtc.net


Library of Congress Cataloging-in-Publication Data

Marcinkowska, Renata, 1965–
    Power drills for team tennis / Renata Marcinkowska.
        p. cm.
    ISBN 0-893009-04-1
    1. Tennis—Training. 2. Tennis teams.  I. Title.

CV 1002.9.T.7 M37 1999

99-056252


Editorial consultants: Nancy Pagett and Phil Rollinson
Consultant for the Charts: Cid Carvalho and Chengyu Sun
Cover by Janet Katz

Printed in the United States of America

*In memory of my mother*

Daniela Marcinkowska

# Table of Contents

# PREFACE

Tennis is very much like chess; if you play it smart, your chances of winning will improve. This manual is designed for all league players as a do-it-yourself coaching manual. Some of the drills are more advanced than others, but all players at every level can profit from them. By spending just five minutes per drill, you can dramatically improve your tennis game and your team's competitiveness, while you have fun in the process. Enjoy!

# INTRODUCTION.
# TEAMS, PARTNERS, AND LEAGUES

## YOUR TEAM.

The first thing to do is to form a team. While assembling your team, it's a good idea to make sure that your players are not separated from each other by more than one level. So, on a 4.0 team, the lowest player should be rated no less than a 3.5, etc. It is also a good idea to try to create a team that is committed to improving. Your players must have the time and the desire to get together at least once a week to practice as a team.

The way some teams set up their players is as follows: the two strongest, two medium strong, two weakest, etc. But there are other formulas, depending on the particular talents and styles of the team's players.

## PARTNERS.

It is a good idea to stick with the same partner. Try to avoid switching partners from week to week. It is best to have one regular partner and one back-up partner, so that you can practice with both, about 75% of the time with your regular partner and 25% with the backup. This way, you are prepared to play with each.

Personal compatibility is very important. You need to get along with and trust your partner. So pick one with whom you are comfortable and are going to enjoy working out.

Your abilities should also complement each other. If you are a powerful player, you need to look for a partner with touch. If you have topspin, look for someone that slices. If you hit from the baseline, look for someone with a big volley, etc. It's fine if you both have the same style of play, e.g., serve and volley. But what you don't want is two players together that hit the ball the same way with the same spin, because your opposition sooner or later will get into a groove and blast you! You want to keep your opponents off balance. That's why partners with different spins work well together.

Once you choose a partner, it's important to develop a feel for each other. You need to heighten your awareness of your partner on the court. The good partner always knows where the other one is. This is something you work on as a team. You need to move together and understand each other's games while on the court.

One important thing to work out with each other is which is your best side on the court, i.e., which one of you returns better from the deuce and which from the ad court. When you and your partner are returning serve, it is important that you return from the same side. Very often people say, "I play both sides depending on what my partner wants." But the fact is that everyone has one side that is better than the other. When you figure out which is the stronger, you should stick with it.

There are two good ways to find out. First, have your partner serve sixty times to you in the deuce court and sixty in the ad. Half of these should go to your forehand and half to your backhand in each court. Your goal is to return an equal number of forehands down the line, down the middle, and crosscourt. Do the same with the backhand. You will probably feel more comfortable and will be more effective on one side than the other; that should be your side.

There is also another way by gauging your instinctive feel for the court. It should be done only once to determine your initial response. Place a can of balls at the corner of the inside alley line and the baseline in both deuce and ad courts. Standing at the net in the center of the court with your back to the net, first look at one of the cans. Close your eyes, then open them and look at it again. Close your eyes again and keeping them closed try to walk straight to that can. Stop and open your eyes when you think you have reached it. Start over and do the same exercise with the other can in the other corner. The can that you get closer to and with less hesitation will indicate which side is right for you.

# LEAGUES.

You should play in a league that is true to your rating. So, if you are a 3.0 player, play 3.0. If you are a 3.5 player, play 3.5. What often happens is that players think that if they play "up" in the competitive season, their quality of play will improve. In one way that's true, but there are always two sides to every coin. If you play up during the competitive season, chances are you are going to lose more often than not, and your confidence will go down. In the long run, this will not help your game, because once you lose your confidence, it's hard to get it back. So, in the competitive season, play at your rated level.

But in order to improve and avoid loss of confidence, play in three or four tournaments during the season at the next higher level. This will give you the extra competition, yet will not ruin your confidence. If you cannot find time to enter tournaments, another option is to schedule three or four matches during the season with people slightly better than you are. If you are 3.0, then play with a team of 3.5 players, etc. This way will give you opportunities to improve at a reasonable pace. If your league has a noncompetitive season, reverse this pattern. Try playing up one level, treating it strictly as practice. Meanwhile, in order not to lose touch with reality, play tournaments and schedule some practice matches at your true level.

# CHAPTER 1.
# WORKING WITH YOUR PARTNER

These drills are aimed at heightening your awareness of each other and helping you both to move together as a team.

## DRILL # 1. Moving Together.

You don't need your racquet for this one, but this drill is very important for getting a feel for your partner.

The idea is to move around the court always keeping the same distance between you and your partner. Take turns leading in this exercise. Start at the baseline and move in unison to the net. Then move from side to the side, making sure that you are not too close together and not too far apart. Switch and let the other be the leader. Repeat for five minutes.

(Take account of your and your partner's size, but don't try to overcompensate, as often happens. Be sure to stay on the same line with your partner no matter what the size difference. If your partner is much shorter than you and tends to play back more toward the service line, you should adjust your position to stay in the same vertical relationship on the court. When playing, after the original position, adjust to the person who is hitting the ball.)

# DRILL # 2. Moving Together in Play.

You will need someone to feed the ball (an extra person on your team). This will turn Drill #1 into a play situation.

With you and your partner starting on the baseline, have the feeder give each of you to return: one approach shot (moving toward the net, **2a**), six volleys, and two overheads (**2b**), so that you practice moving together back and forth without crowding or running into each other.

# Drill 2 Moving Together in Play (2a)

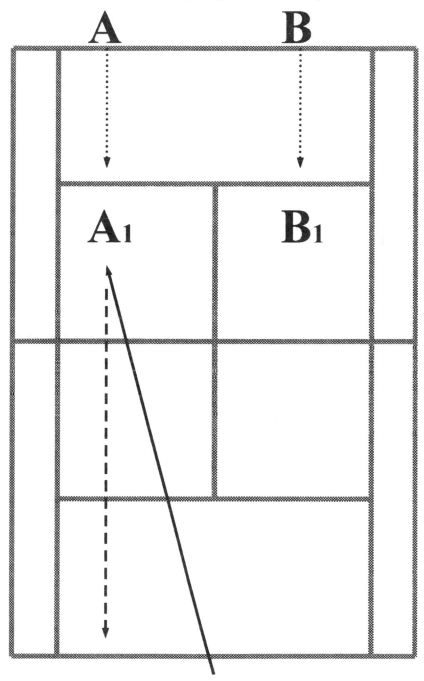

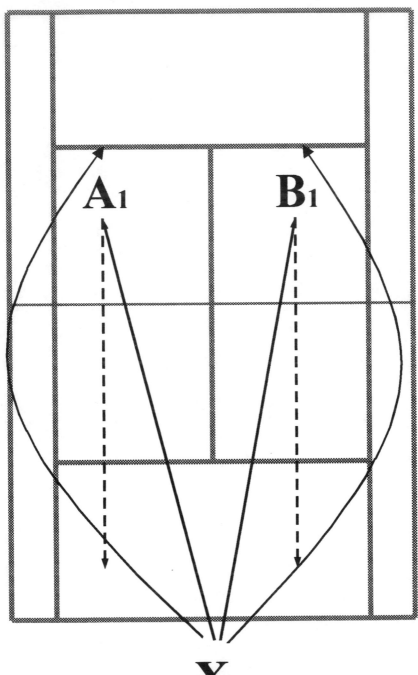

# DRILL # 3. Switching and Covering.

Good partners not only move well together but switch to cover for each other (a feeder is required).

Have your feeder hit a high floater down the left center. **B** hits the ball and continues to slide into the deuce court, while **A** crosses behind to cover the baseline in the ad court (**3a**). Then **A** is fed an approach shot and comes to the net (**3b**). Next the feeder hits six to eight volleys and overheads with **A** and **B** at the net (**3c**). (This is considered one set.) Reverse the drill with **A** and **B** changing positions. Each player does four sets from the deuce and ad courts.

# Drill 3 Switching and Covering (3a)

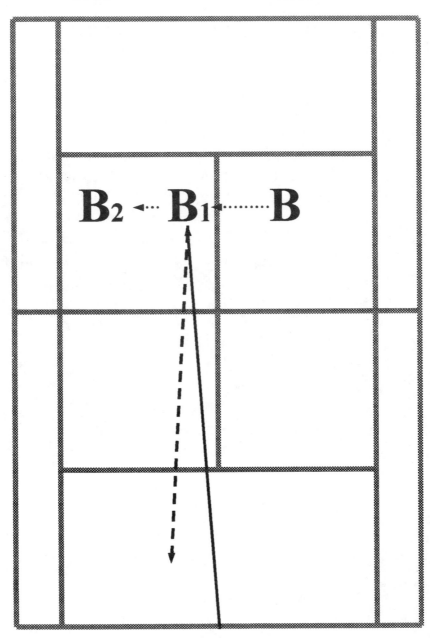

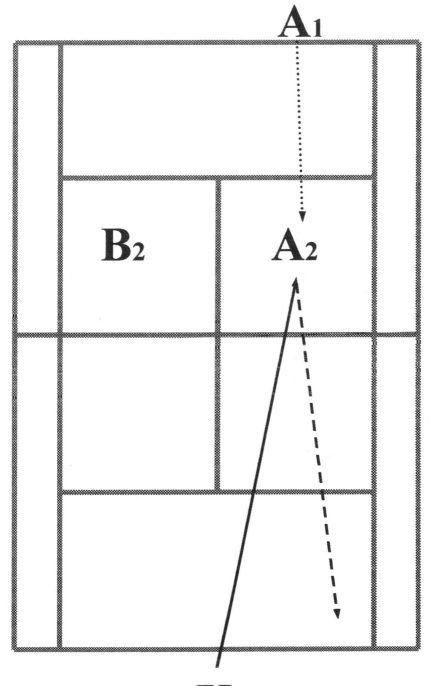

3b

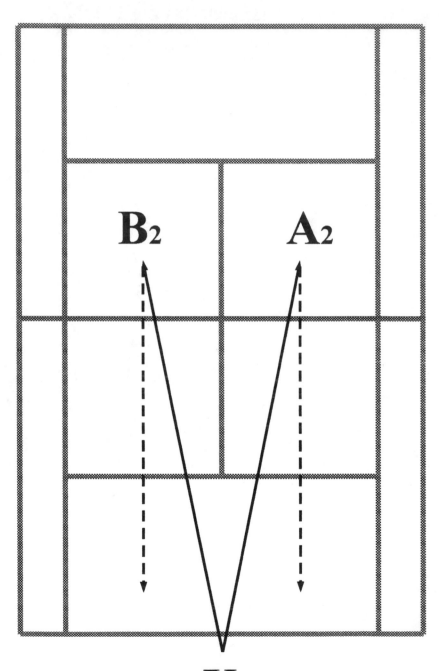

3c

## DRILL # 4. Up and Back.

This is an up-and-back drill for two teams working in a situation that happens very often at the 3.0 and 3.5 levels.

From the baseline **A** and **D** keep hitting deep crosscourt shots to each other (**4a**), while **B** and **C** try to poach and switch (**4b**). Remember, in this situation, the sole purpose of the baseline partner is to set up the net partner. You should always try to hit into your opponent's body on the baseline. This way your shot will take away the possibility of angled returns and at the same time give your net partner a better opportunity to poach.

If you get stuck on the baseline, make sure you hit as deep as possible in order to give your partner at the net time to decide whether or not to poach. When your partner does poach, be sure to cover the half of the court left vacant.

# Drill 4 Up-and-Back (4a)

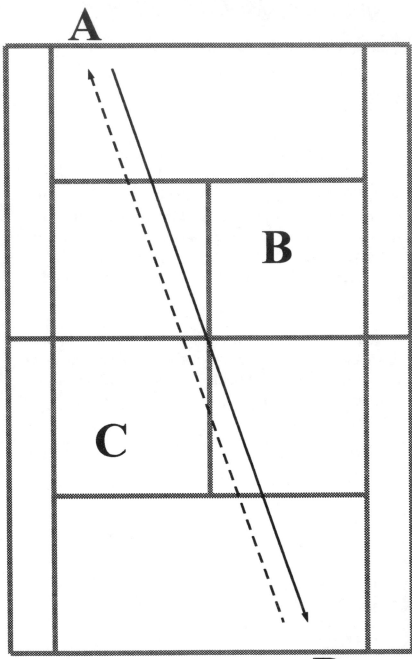

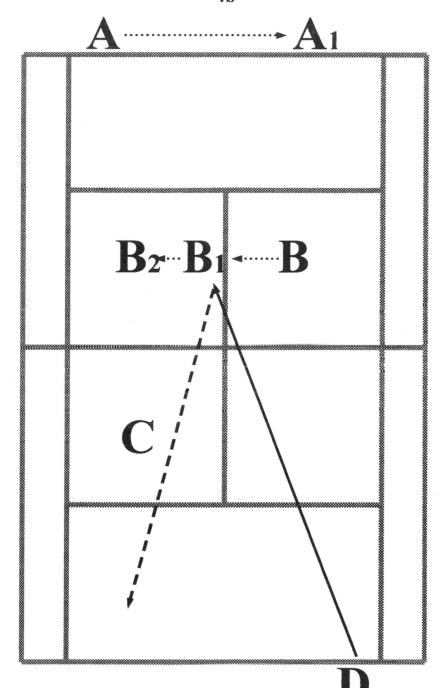

# DRILL # 5. Covering at the Net.

(A feeder is needed.) The point of this is to practice moving together at the net.

Both partners are at the net. The feeder lobs over **A**. **B** runs behind and returns the ball while **A** switches (**5a**). The feeder's approach shot then brings **B** to the net taking the spot vacated by **A** and returning a volley (**5b**). Continue the drill with the feeder lobbing over **B** and **A** running behind to return from the baseline and **B** shifting to cover. The feeder then gives an approach shot bringing **A** to the net. Repeat the sequence six times. Then with **A** and **B** both at the net have the feeder end the drill with six to eight volleys to be returned (**5c**).

# Drill 5 Covering at the Net (5a)

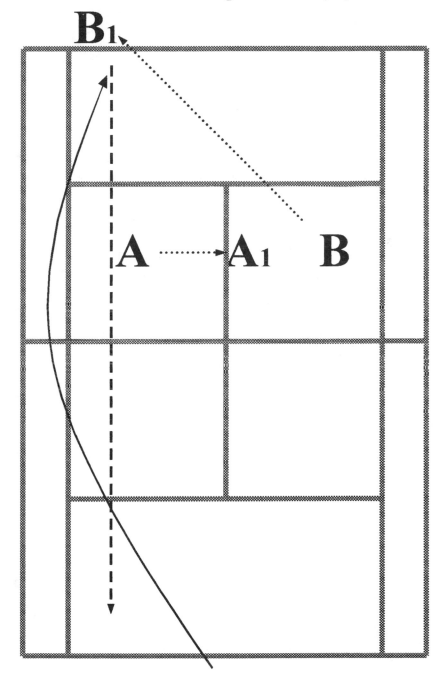

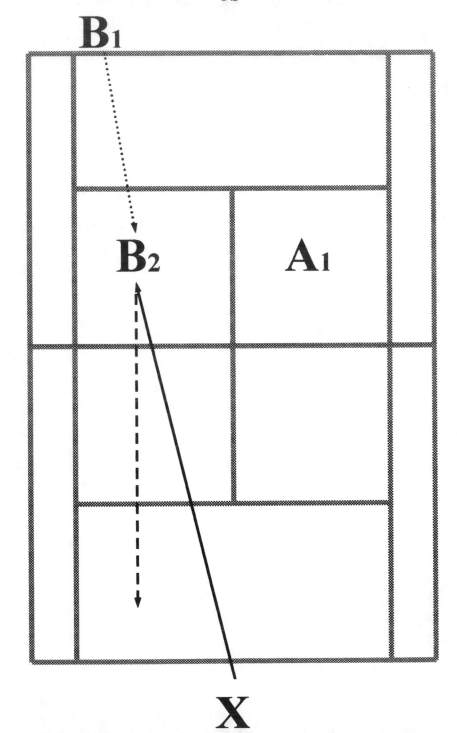

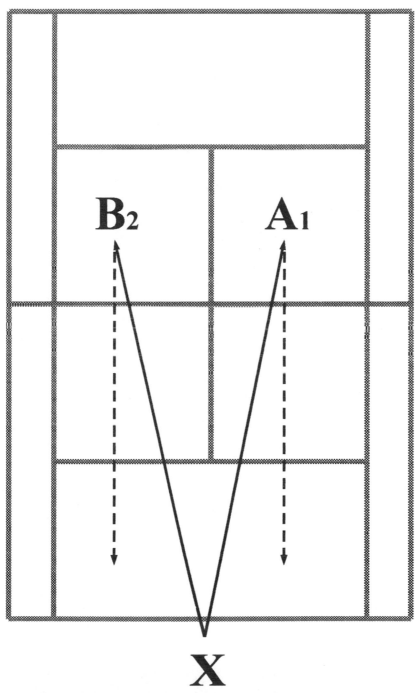

# CHAPTER 2.
# BASIC INSTINCTS:
# POSITION, SERVE, AND RETURN

By positioning yourself correctly, you can get an edge even before the point begins.

When your partner is serving and you are at the net, don't hug the alley. The proper position for you in relationship to the alley depends on your reach. From the ready position, crossover with your foot and stretch across your body with your racquet toward the alley. Your racquet should reach to about a foot and a half from the outside line. For vertical positioning between the net and the service line, you should stand anywhere from halfway to two-thirds of the way back from the net. Of course, once your partner serves, you can return to your regular position.

When your team is returning serve, the partner at the net should not only watch the service line to help call the serves in or out, but also watch the opposition's net person on the first ball and be prepared for a poaching shot on the return. The minute your partner returns the serve past the opposition's net player, you move to your regular position closer to the net.

Ideally, the server should always try to set up the partner at the net. Therefore, service placement and percentages are extremely important. Work on your service accuracy. When serving from the deuce court, serve down the middle or into the body as much as possible. Occasionally hit to the forehand side to keep your opponents honest. Serving in the ad court, you can spread out your shots more evenly, but here too the best serve to set up your partner at the net is into your opponent's body. Jam them, and their returns will frequently be floaters down the middle. Instead of aiming directly at them when you serve, hit slightly toward the center line on both sides. That way, you will still crowd them but will hit to their backhand in the deuce court and their forehand in the ad court. This will limit their ability to hit a return down the line on either side and allow your net partner to concentrate on poaching.

# DRILL # 1. Being Ready at the Net.

The best way to simulate this situation while working on your positioning in serve, return, and net play is as follows.

**A** serves (but **D** doesn't return that ball; the serve is strictly for practice). **D** hits out of the hopper as if returning the serve with a shot down the middle. **B** crosses and hits at **C**'s feet, while **A** comes in and takes **B**'s spot at the net (**1a**); **D** feeds one ball to **A**, who will hit at **C**'s feet (**1b**). Then **D** will feed six more high balls to **A** and **B** at the net (**1b**). They will concentrate on hitting only at **C**'s feet. **C**'s only concern is to get the ball back in play, and each point should be played out, allowing **A** and **B** to work on positioning as well as crossing and switching. The drill is completed when each player has been in each position for five minutes per position.

# Drill 1 Being Ready at the Net (1a)

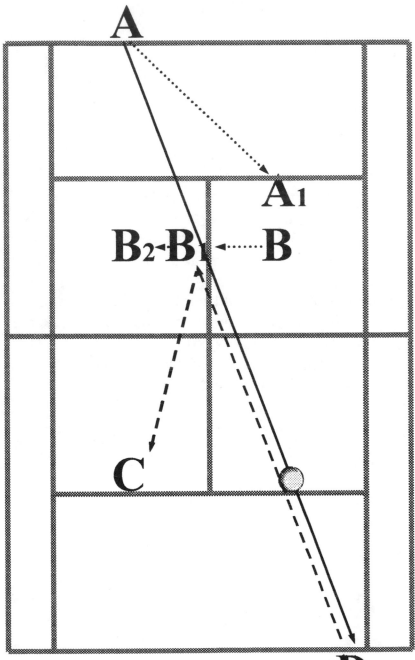

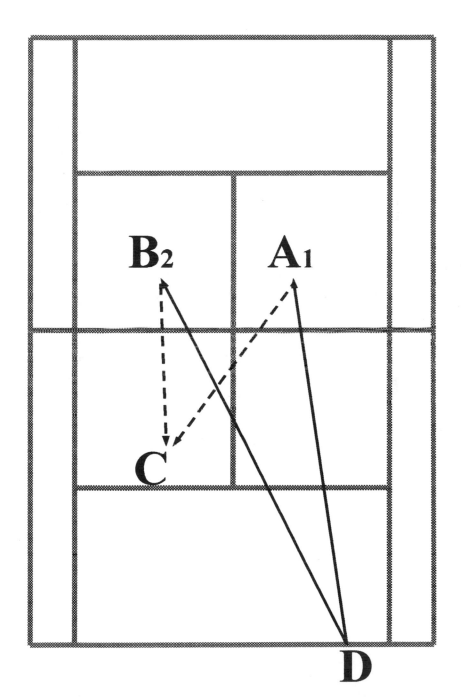

## DRILL # 2. Responding to the Second Serve.

If your opponents serve and stay back, make sure that you hit an aggressive return and follow it up to the net. If the next shot coming back to you is below the level of the net, you should hit it to the opponent farthest back from the net. If the shot is above the level of the net cord, hit it at the feet of the opponent closest to the net or go between the two. To practice this strategy, use this drill.

Everybody serves four times, using second serves only. Returners must come into the net, and then the point is played out.

**A** serves a second serve to **D**. **D** returns and comes to the net (**2a**). **C** and **D** try to isolate the net player, **B**, hitting at **B**'s feet, or they hit between **A** and **B** (**2b**). Four serves each. Drill is complete when each player has served from both sides.

## Drill 2 Responding to the Second Serve (2a)

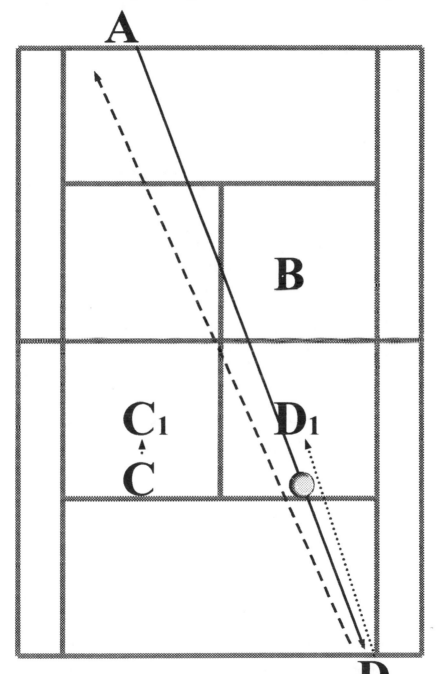

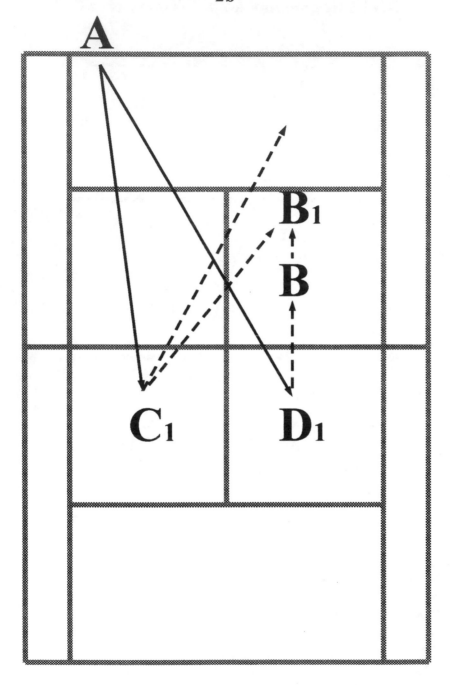

# DRILL # 3. Serving Offensively.

Server has to come into the net on both serves, first from the deuce and then from the ad court.

**A** serves to **D** and moves aggressively to the net to volley (**3a**). **A** and **B** try to isolate **C** at the net and hit at **C**'s feet (**3b**); repeat from the ad side. Rotate: four serves each from each player. Points are played out from both sides.

# Drill 3 Serving Offensively (3a)

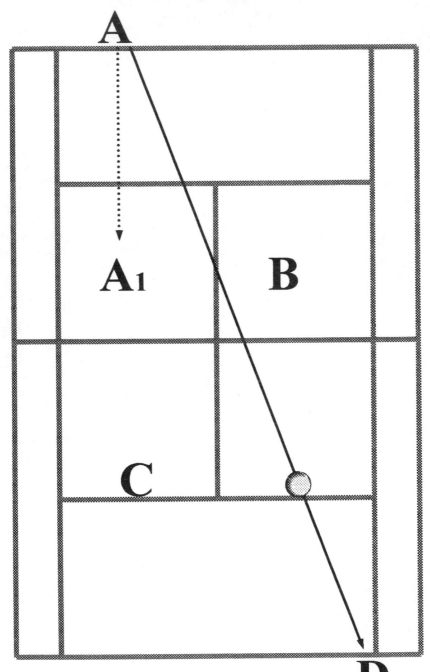

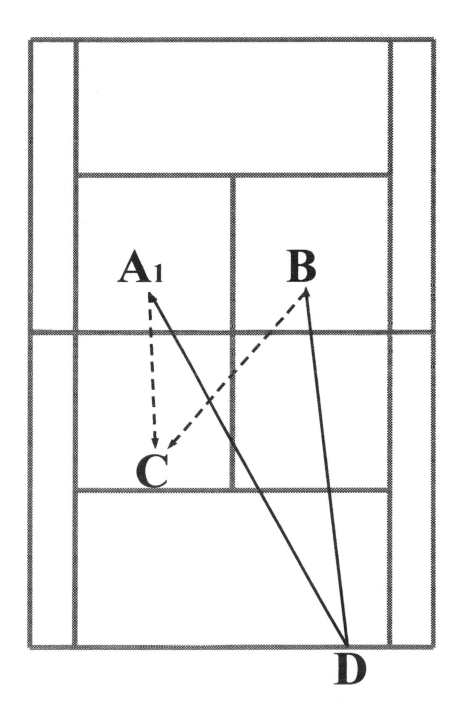

## DRILL # 4. Serving Offensively and Defensively.

A serves from the deuce and ad courts. **B** must cross on both serves. The server will either come in to the net as the net player crosses to poach (**4a**) or will move across the back court (**4b**) Rotate: four serves for each player from both service sides. Points are played out .

# Drill 4 Serving Offensively and Defensively (4a)

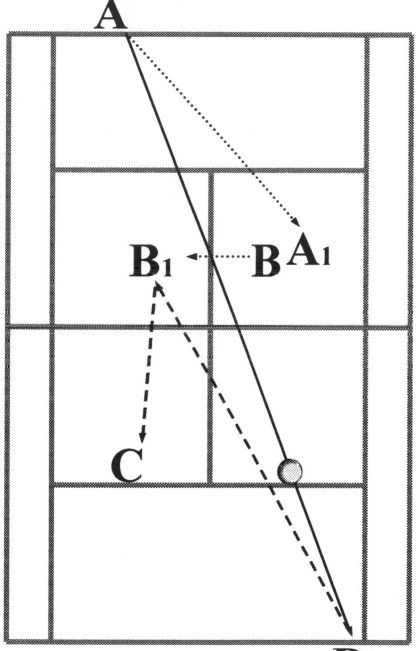

**4b**

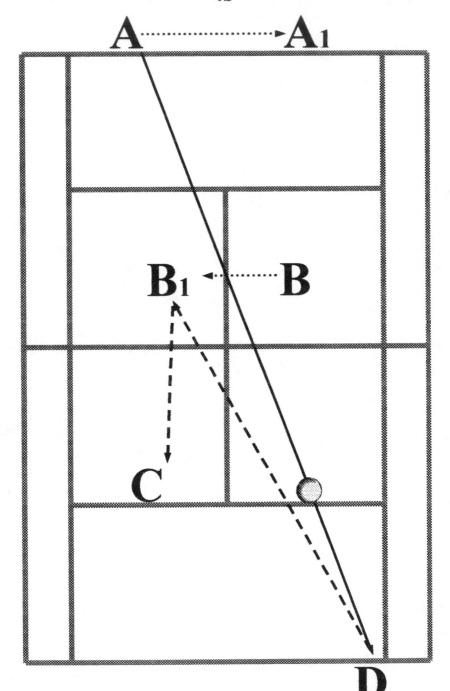

## DRILL # 5. Returns Down the Alley.

Returners hit down the alleys. Returner must go down the line with the first ball. Anything goes after that.

**A** serves to **D**, who returns down the alley. Play points out from both service sides. Rotate: four serves for each player from deuce and ad sides.

## Drill 5 Returns Down the Alley

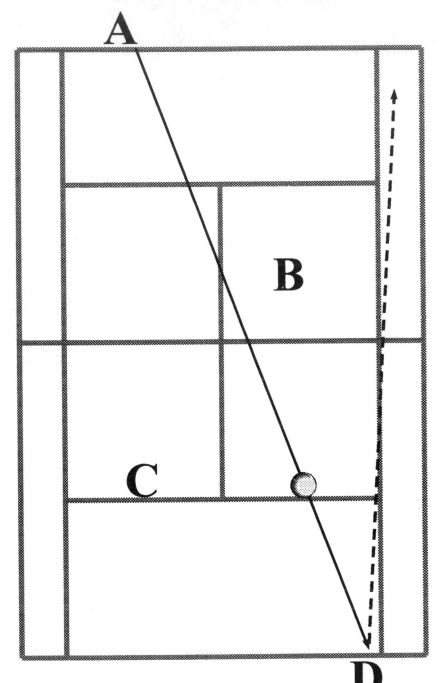

# DRILL # 6. Lobs and Switching.

Returner lobs over the opponent's net player and comes to the net. In this drill, even if it is a poor lob, the player at the net should let it go by. The purpose is to practice switching techniques. After each lob, play the points out.

**A** serves to **D**, who lobs over **B** and comes to the net, while **A** covers on the baseline and **B** shifts to the deuce court (**6a**). **A** returns the lob and play continues (**6b**). Four serves for each player in deuce and ad courts.

# Drill 6 Lobs and Switching (6a)

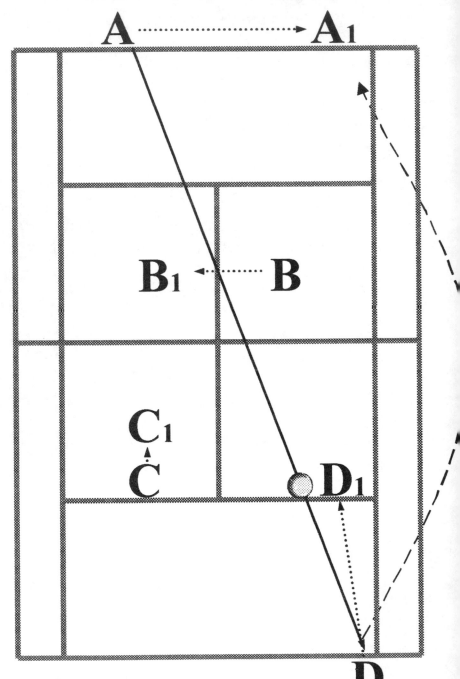

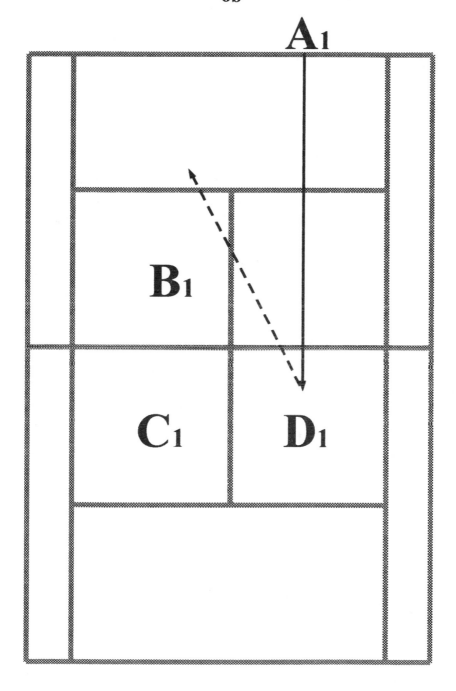

## DRILL # 7.  Placing Returns.

Here the returner works on placement. (Play the points out.)

**A** serves and comes in. **D** must either return down the middle, splitting **A** and **B** (**7a**) or hit a short ball no further than the service line and preferably at the feet of **A** or **B** (**7b**). Once **D** returns, anything goes. Repeat with **A** serving from the ad court to **C**. Rotate with four serves for each player from both sides of the court.

## Drill 7 Placing Returns (7a)

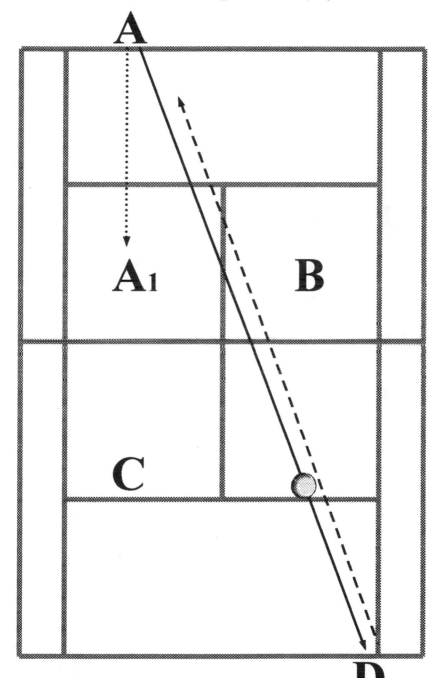

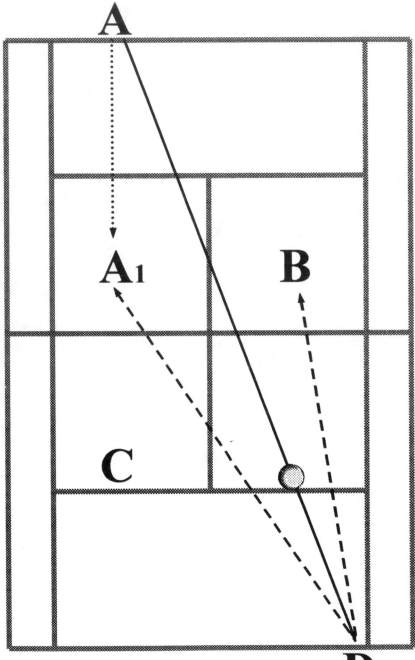

# DRILL # 8. Getting Off the Baseline.

This is a very important drill that simulates a situation where you and your partner are on the defensive. Your partner is up at the net, while you are stuck in the back court, and both opposition players are aggressively at the net. You have three legitimate options to keep your partner from being killed at the net and to give you the opportunity to come aggressively to the net. (1) Hit a low volley to either of your opponents' forehand, so that the shot has to be dug out. The forehand is preferable because it is not as natural a shot as the backhand. (2) Hit a bullet, as hard as you can, directly at either opponent's body (3) Hit a lob over either opponent to the backhand side, forcing the more difficult backhand overhead.

To begin the drill, the server **D** stays back; **A** returns and comes to the net. On the next shot, **D** uses one of the three choices: a low volley (**8a**); bullet to the body (**8b**); or lob to the backhand side (**8c**). Each player takes turns serving four times from the deuce and ad side, and choosing which of the three options to try. Play the points out.

If you want to work on one of these particular shots, keep track of your points, but give the shot that you all agree to practice a premium. Make it worth 2 points when executed correctly. Play to 11 points total with four serves each from each player on both sides.

# Drill 8 Getting Off the Baseline (8a)

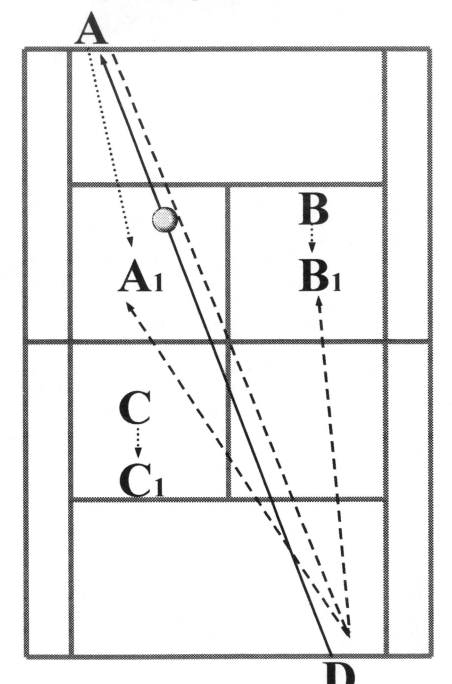

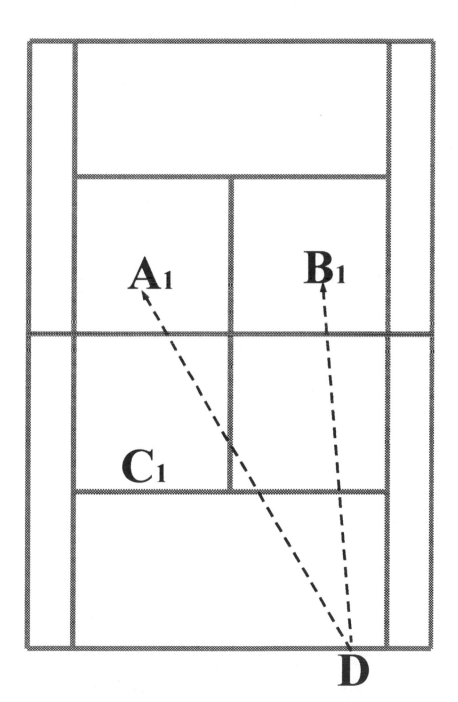

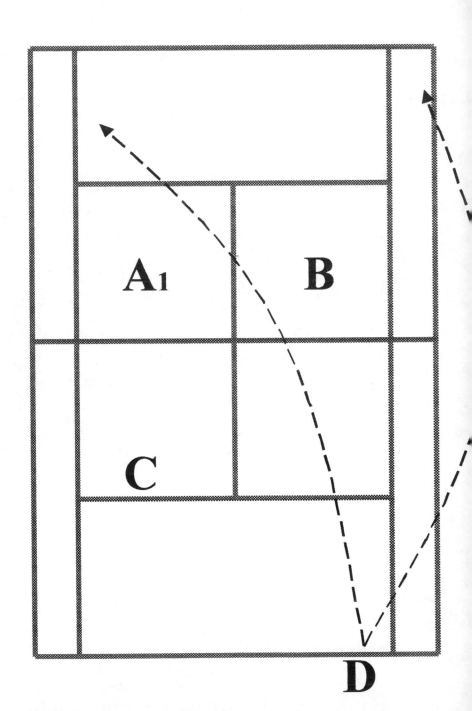

## SUGGESTIONS.

When poaching, some people use hand signals. If that is what works best for you and your partner, that's great. Other players go strictly by intuition, and there is nothing wrong with that. When a very aggressive partner is at the net, the server should indicate ahead of time where the serve is going, but not the reverse. Nothing ruins a server's confidence quicker than for the net player to indicate where to serve.

For the net player, if you decide to poach, don't hesitate and return to your regular position; just do it. Hesitation can shake your and your partner's confidence. It is better to lose a couple of points playing aggressively, because in the long run it pays off with the trust of your partner (it will also rattle your opposition.)

## AUSTRALIAN POSITION.

Remember to stand closer to the center when you serve. Playing Australian can be a good addition to your game. First, it can nullify your opponents' strengths. For example, if they have a great crosscourt return, put your net player on your side of the court. Secondly, the Australian position can compensate for having an off day with one of your shots. If your backhand is off and you are serving to the ad side, put your net partner on that side at the net. Conversely, if your forehand is suffering on a particular day and you are serving from the deuce side, put your partner at the net on that side. Finally, shifting into the Australian position on an important point can surprise and make your opponents tentative about what shot to make.

In a match situation, unless your second serve is extremely good, only try Australian on the first serve. You and your partner should practice your serves and returns on a regular basis in Australian, as well as, of course, in your normal position. A good way to do this is to alternate practicing placement and power. If you practice twice a week, practice placement on one day and power on the other.

The drills for Australian serving are the same as for regular serving.

## Australian Position: A to Serve

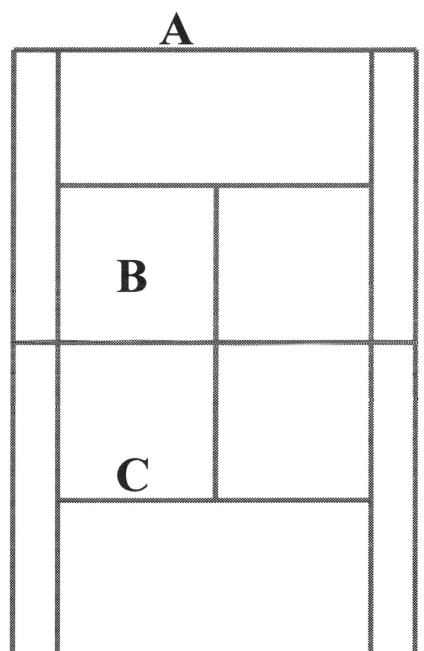

## DRILL # 9. Serving and Volleying in the Australian Position.

A serves to D and comes to the net. Play the points out. Each player serves four times from both service sides.

## DRILL # 10. Staying Back in the Australian Position.

A serves and stays back, moving to cover at the baseline. D returns to A and comes in. The point is played out. Four serves for each player, practicing Australian from both sides.

# Drill 9 Serving and Volleying in the Australian Position

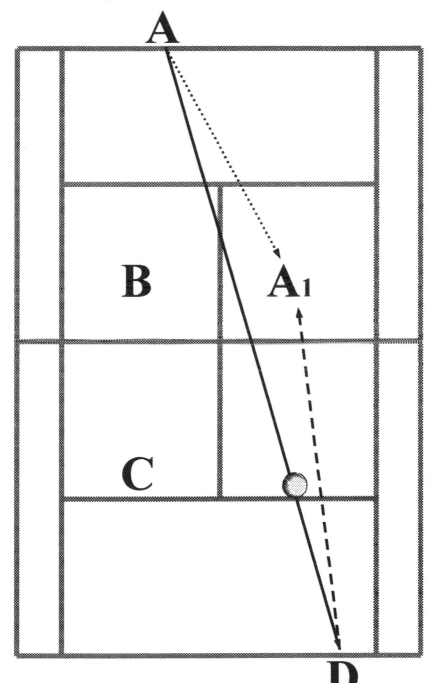

# Drill 10 Staying Back in the Australian Position

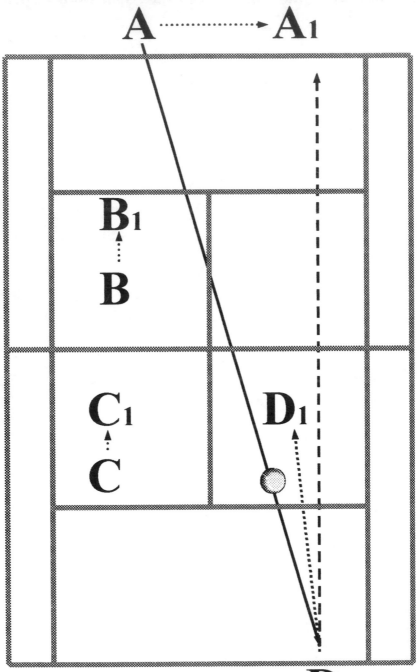

# CHAPTER 3.
# IMPROVING YOUR REACTION TIME (DRILLS FOR FOUR OR MORE PLAYERS)

How often have you found yourself in a situation where your partner hits a floater or a short lob and your opponents hit it back down your throat? They either take it as an aggressive volley, or kill it as an overhead. Most likely, you turn around and try to get out of the way. But your turning away gives your opponents extra confidence, while yours slips away. With fast hands, you can have a good chance of getting some of these shots back. The next few drills concentrate on improving your reaction time with your hands. They are designed as offensive-defensive routines so that you can practice both.

# DRILL # 1. Basic Four.

(A feeder is required.)

Players **A** and **B** are fed high volleys or overheads; they work on controlling the placement of their shots by practicing hitting at **C** and **D**'s feet. **C** and **D** work on reacting with quick hands and reflexes returning these shots. Continue for five minutes. Then, making sure to hit only inside the singles court lines, play out the points; the first team to 10 wins. Reverse the team roles and repeat the procedure. Finally, expand to hitting inside the doubles lines and repeat the drill.

# Drill 1 Basic Four

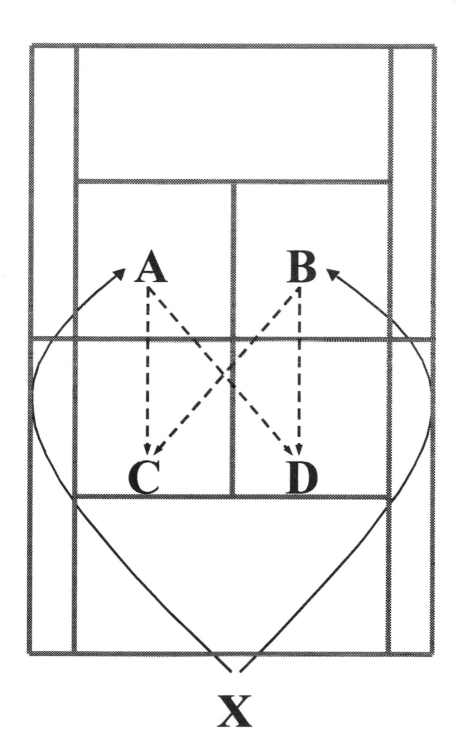

# DRILL # 1A.

This is a variation of the same drill but designed for 8 players. Only one ball is in play at a time.

**A/B** and **G/H** can only hit lobs, and they should try to make them as good as possible so that the net players cannot kill the shots (**1Aa**). At the net **C/D** and **E/F** can only move back as far as the service line, but no further. When **E** or **F** get an overhead they can hit, they go for the feet of **C** and **D**, who move back to the service line to return, practicing their fast hands (**1Ab**). After they hit the ball, they move up closer to the net again, and the process starts over. Rotate positions clockwise after 4 balls so that everyone gets to play in each position.

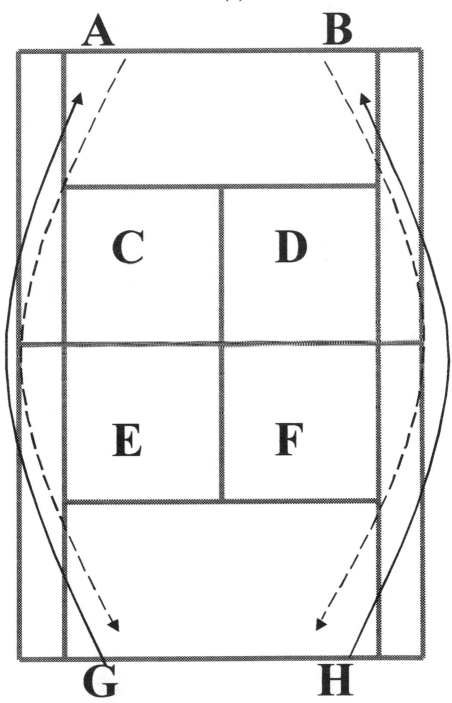

1A (b)

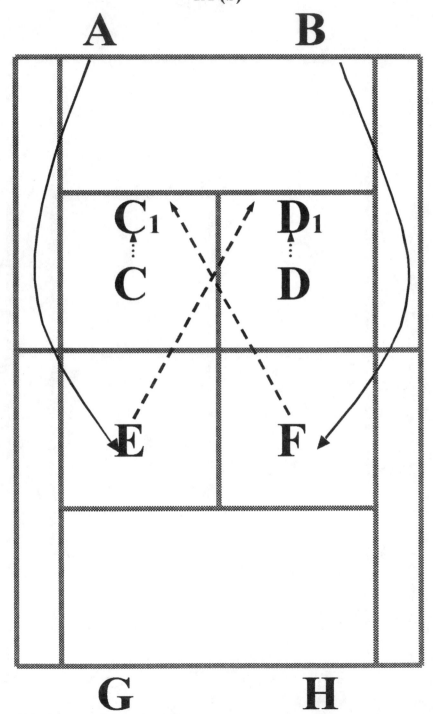

## DRILL # 1B.

This is a variation for 6 players. Only one ball in play.

**A** and **B** alternate working on deep lobs, while **C** and **D** try to work on volleys, and **E** and **F** try either to lob or pass **C** and **D** (**1Ba**). If **E** and **F** hit a successful lob over **C** and **D**, they come in and **C** and **D** then move back to the service line and exercise fast hands (**1Bb**). Play the points out; first team to 10 wins; then teams switch positions.

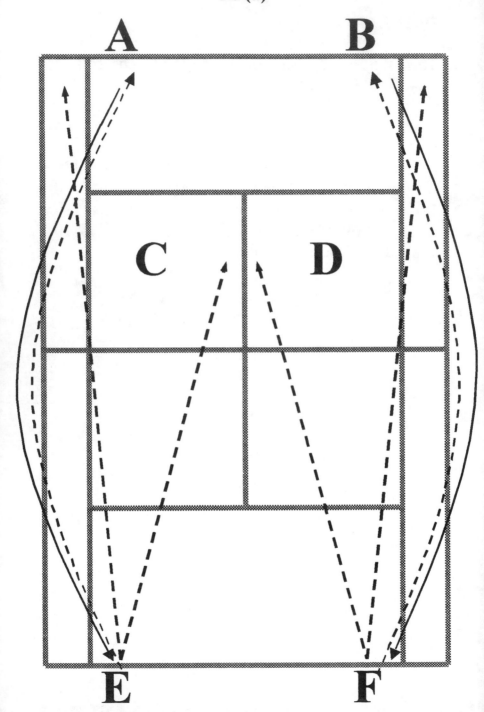

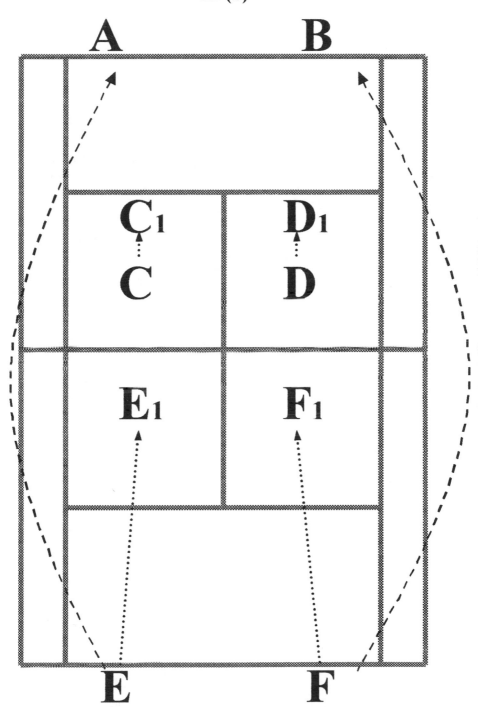

# DRILL  # 2. Offensive Drill for Four.

(A feeder is required.)

A and B are up, and the feeder alternates hitting low volleys first to one, then to the other (2a). The moment that A or B make contact with the ball from the feeder, C and D move up to duke it out at the net (2b). Play out the points in the singles court lines only. First side to 10 wins; switch sides and repeat. Expand to the doubles lines and repeat the drill.

# Drill 2 Offensive Drill for Four (2a)

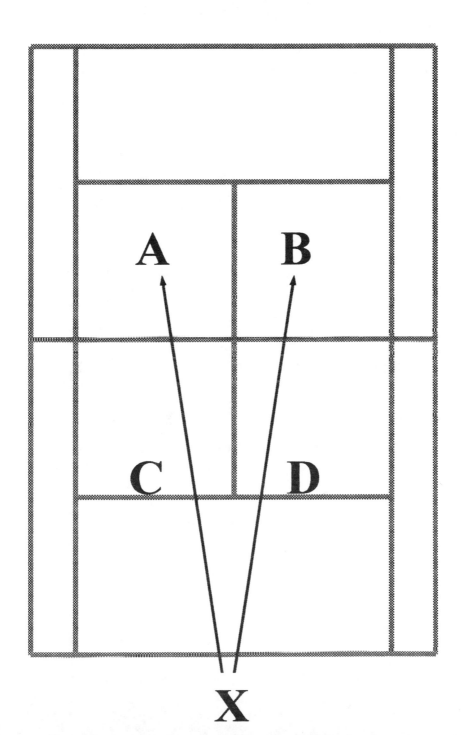

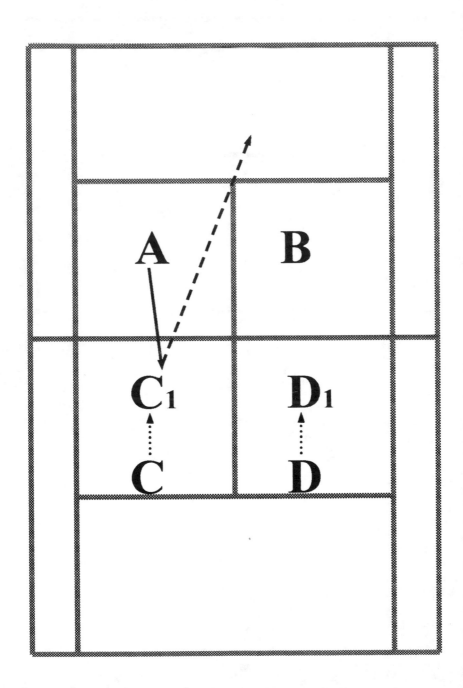

**DRILL # 3. Defense to Offense.**

Drill for four (feeder required).

This time **A** and **B** are up and start off on defense; they alternately get a ball at their feet as a half volley from the feeder. **C** and **D** aggressively move in as soon as **A** or **B** makes contact with the ball to contest the point. **C** and **D** try to pick up the volley and hopefully nail it in between **A** and **B** at the "T" of the court. First side to 10 wins; then teams switch positions and repeat.

# Drill 3 Defense to Offense

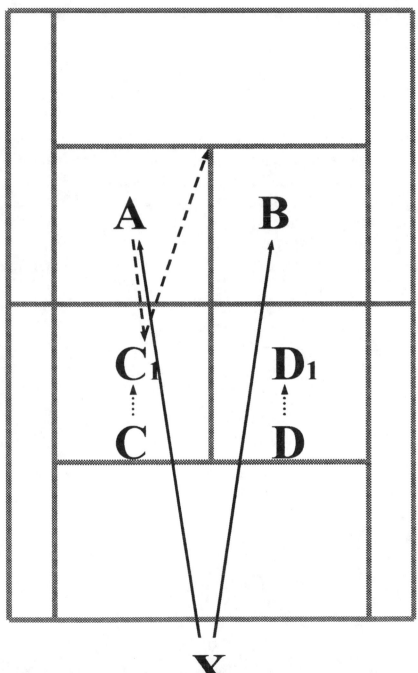

# DRILL  # 4. Moving with the Ball.

This drill for four is designed to help you move with your partner as the ball pulls you wide on the court. Play the points out.

**A** and **B** are up; they have 4 balls in their pockets, or as many as they can handle (have a hopper on the side). First, **B** hits to **C** wide. **C** returns as **A** moves to cover down the line with **B** following to the left to cover the center; **D** also moves to cover the center (**4a**). In the second point, **A** feeds to the alley wide to **D**. As **D** gets it and returns, **C** covers the middle at the baseline and **A** covers the center at the net (**4b**). Repeat this sequence to 10 points. Then teams switch positions and repeat the drill.

# Drill 4 Moving with the Ball (4a)

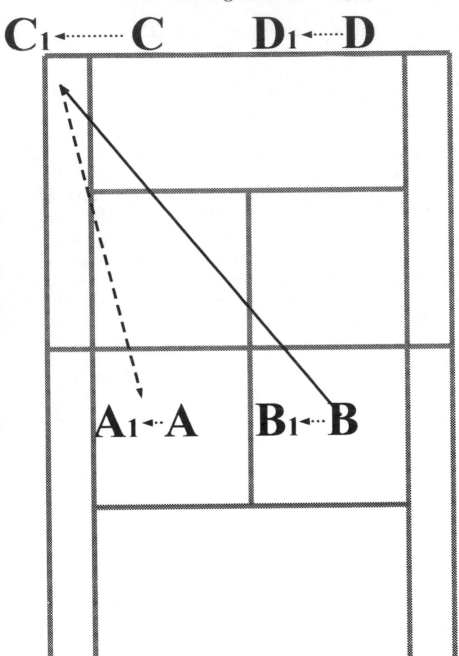

**4b**

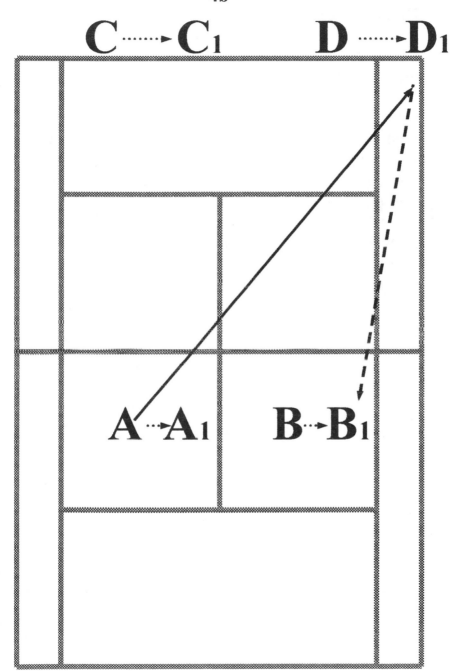

## DRILL # 4A.

This is a variation using a one-up and one-back situation. Play the points out.

**A** and **B** are up. Again **B** hits wide to **C**. **A** and **B** again shift to the left, while **C** returns trying to hit either a passing shot down the line, crosscourt, or in between **A** and **B** (**4Aa**). In the second point **A** hits wide to **D**. **A** and **B** shift to the right while **D** tries a passing shot down the line, crosscourt, or in between **A** and **B** on the return (**4Ab**). Repeat this sequence to 10 points. Then teams switch positions and repeat the drill.

## Drill 4A One-Up and One-Back 4A(a)

$C_1$ ⋯ $C$

$D_1$ ◄⋯ $D$

$A_1$ ⋯ $A$     $B_1$ ⋯ $B$

**4A(b)**

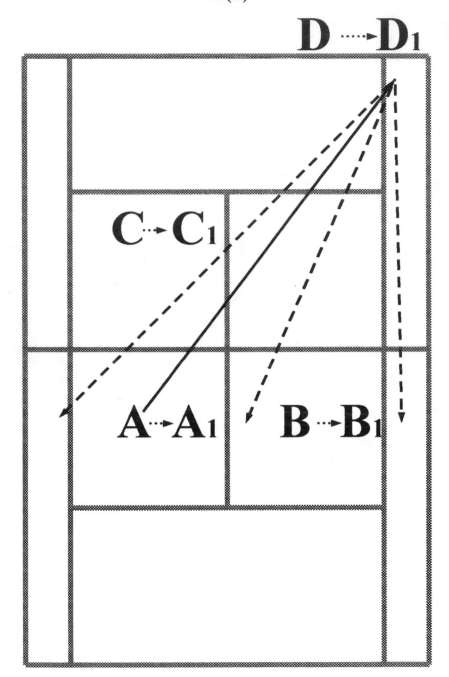

## DRILL # 5. Moving from the Baseline Together.

All four players at the baseline. Play the points out.

**A** feeds the ball alternately to **C** and **D**. The ball should hit the court no more than a yard behind the service line. As soon as the ball bounces and play commences (**5a**), both teams should attempt to come to the net (**5b**). Play first to 10, then switch and repeat with **D** feeding alternately to **A** and **B**.

# Drill 5 Moving from the Baseline Together (5a)

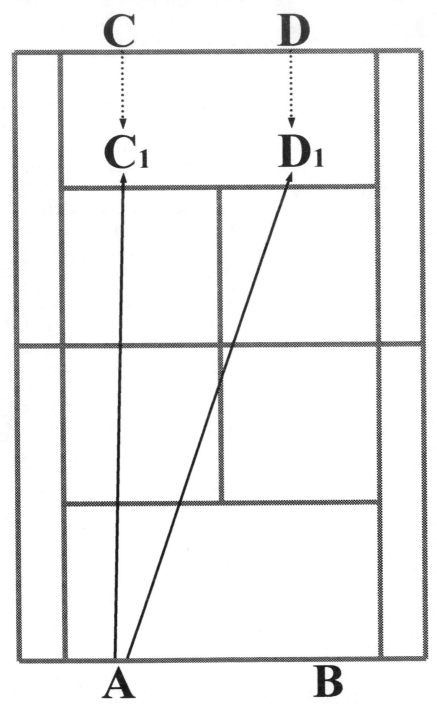

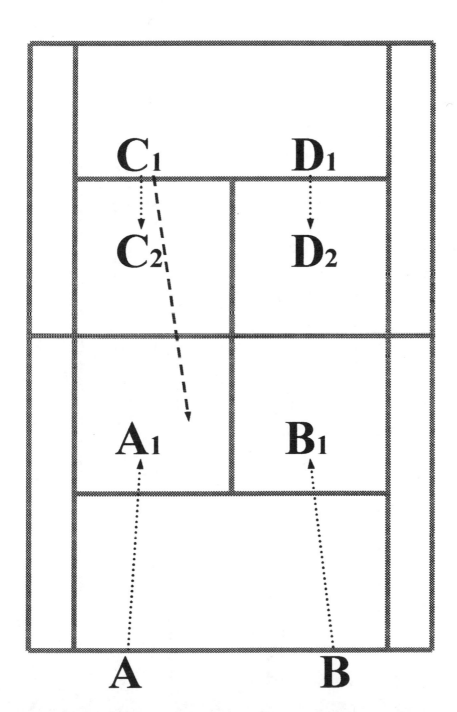

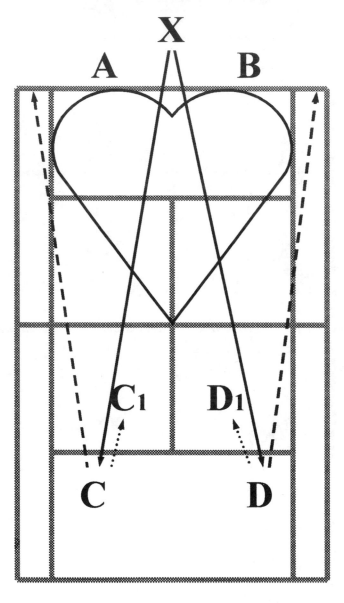

# THE HEART OF THE COURT.

Even though it is important to hit in between players and at their feet, sometimes this tactic will not work, especially if your opponents are very aggressive. In this situation you may end up hitting to your opponents more often than you should. Here are some drills to help you avoid doing just that. The point is to keep your shots away from the "heart" of the court. Go for the angles and the corners at the baseline, as well as the top of the heart, the center baseline. This will help you learn to keep the ball away from your opponents.

## DRILL # 6. Avoiding the Heart.

This drill is called the "Kings of the Court" game (for at least 8 players) A feeder is needed. Here the players work on their feel for the court by avoiding the heart and concentrating on hitting angles, alleys, corners, and the center baseline. All points are played out.

**A** and **B** start on the baseline behind the heart; **C** and **D** are at mid-court, and extra teams of two (**E/F** and **G/H**) are lined up at the baseline behind them. From the baseline behind **A** and **B**, an approach shot is fed to **C** or **D**, and the point is played out. **C** and **D** try to avoid hitting to the heart of the court (**6a**). If **C** and **D** win the first point, the feeder (**X**) hits them another ball; they must win these two points in a row. If they lose either point, then the next team (**E/F**) takes their place, and they line up behind **G** and **H** at the baseline. The fun begins when **C** and **D** (or whichever team) win two straight points. As soon as they win those two points, they run around to the opposite court as fast as they can to take the place of **A** and **B**, who go to the other side and line up behind **G** and **H** waiting their turn (**6b**). While **C** and **D** are running to their new position, a high lob is fed to the new team, **E** and **F**, taking their place (**6c**). This lob must drop and be returned by them before they come to the net and try to win two points in a row, so they can take the place of **C** and **D**. (The only time a lob is hit by the feeder is when the players are switching courts; all other feeds are approach shots and volleys.) Continue play until the feeder runs out of balls in the hopper (just an ordinary hopper available in sports stores is fine; it holds about 70 balls). The team that successfully moves from the **C/D** to the **A/B** positions the most times wins; these players are the kings of the court.

**6b**

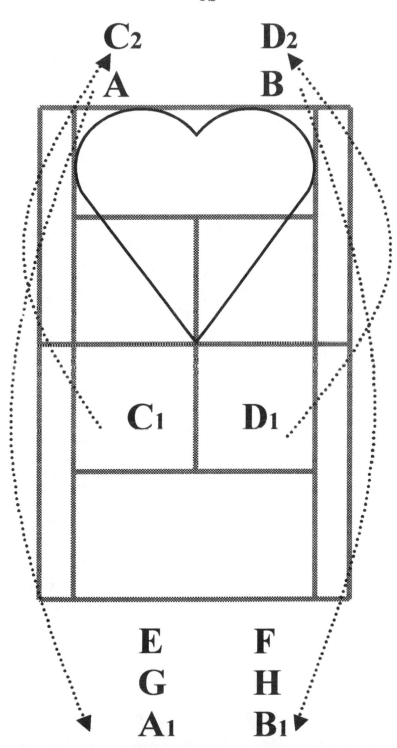

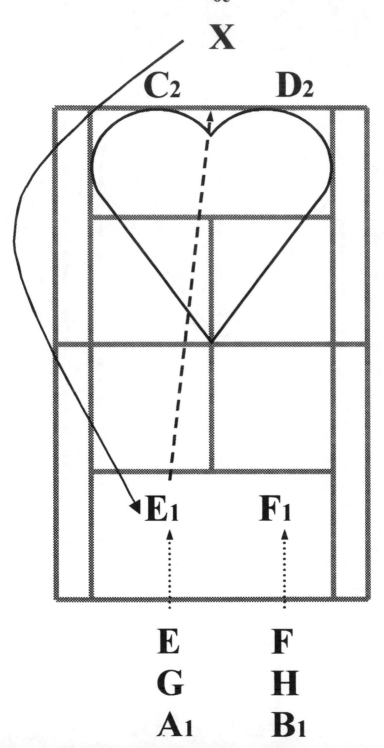

# DRILL # 7. Hitting Down the Alley.

Play the points out.

**A** and **B** are up; **C** and **D** are back. **A** hits the ball to **C**'s forehand. **C** has to return down the alley, and then anything goes. **B** starts again by hitting to **D**'s backhand with **D** returning down the alley. Continue until one side gets 10 points; then switch sides and repeat the drill.


# DRILL # 8. Down the Middle.

Again **A** and **B** are up. **A** hits to **C**. **C** must return the first ball to the middle; then anything goes. **B** hits to **D**, who returns down the middle. First to 10 and switch sides.


# DRILL # 9. Alley and Middle.

Alternate starting play just as in Drills 7 and 8.

**C** and **D** try to play head games with **A** and **B**, who are at the net, by either going down the middle first, to open up the alleys, or vice versa. First to 10 and then switch.

# Drill 7 Hitting Down the Alley

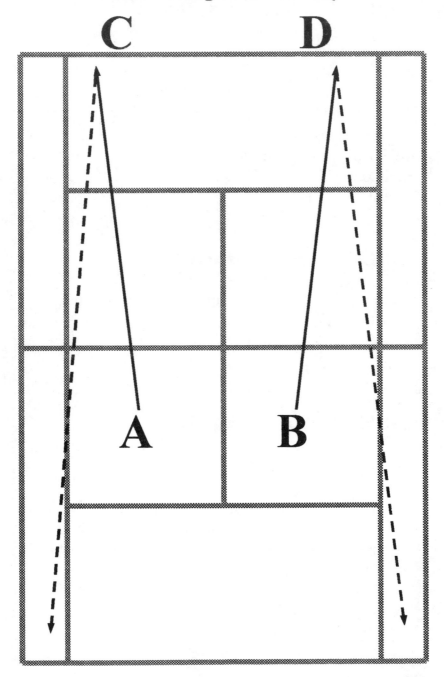

# Drill 8 Down the Middle

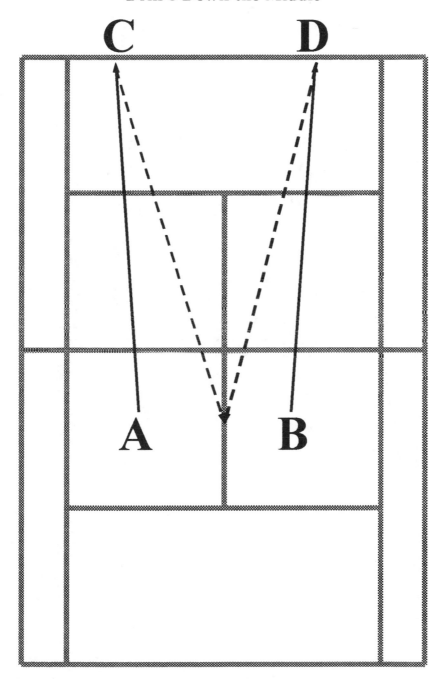

# Drill 9 Alley and Middle

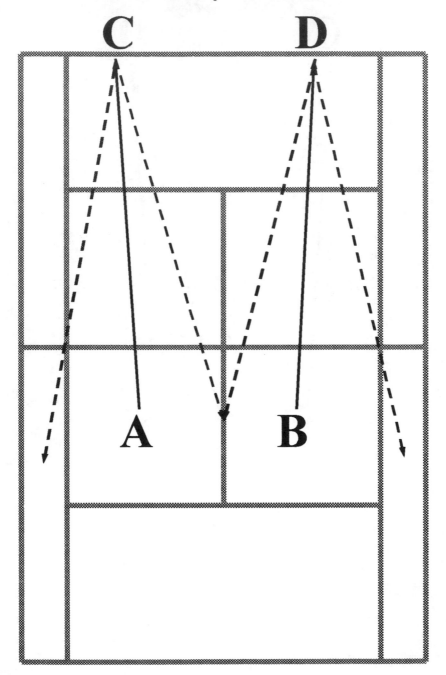

# DRILL # 9A. Penalizing Net Errors.

In this variation, each team is still playing first to 10. The only difference is that whichever team hits the ball into the net loses 2 points instead of 1. The penalty will heighten awareness of the net and improve consistency.

# DRILL # 9B. Penalizing Long and Wide Shots.

Again, each team is playing to 10. But here balls hit wide or long count 2 points. This drill will help the big hitters better their aim by concentrating on their perception of the court. The same is true for those who constantly "spray" the balls. Basically, you need to train yourself to envision a smaller court.

# DRILL # 9C. Offensive Reward.

Same drill; still first to 10. However, in this drill you reward yourselves 2 points for hitting a clean winner, a shot that your opponents don't even touch. This is a good drill for teams that want to improve the power in their game, because it will help focus attention on hitting winners. It will also help the slower moving players, giving them an incentive to run harder and faster to avoid losing those 2 points. So, this drill will also help you develop speed.

## DRILL # 10. Winning at the Net.

In this drill the team at the net works on either isolating and going at the feet of the up opponent or going between the up and back players.

**A** and **B** are up and back; **C** and **D** are at the net. **A** feeds alternately to **C** and **D**. The first return from **C** or **D** has to go to **A**, the back player, and must hit behind the service line (**10a**). **C** and **D** then concentrate on hitting **A**'s return at the feet of **B** or in between **A** and **B** (**10b** and **10c**). After that anything goes. Play four balls and then rotate positions, **B** switching with **A**, etc., until everyone has played out four balls in every position.

# Drill 10 Winning at the Net (10a)

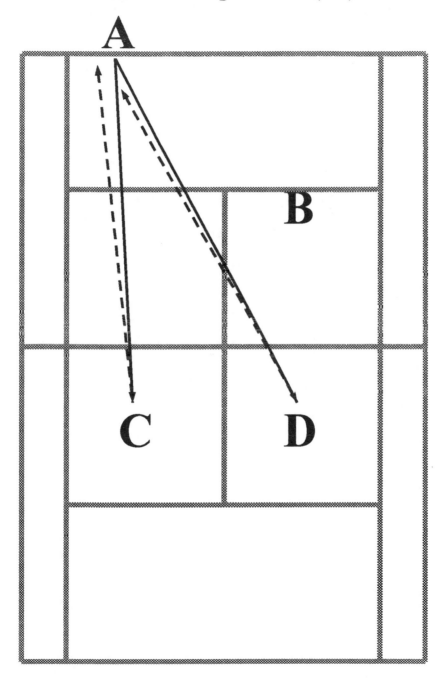

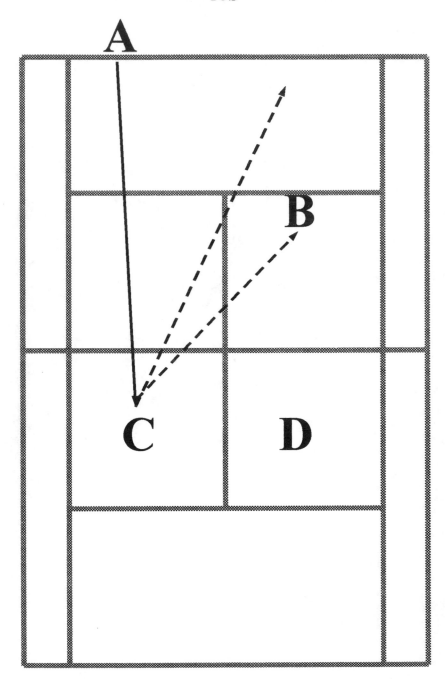

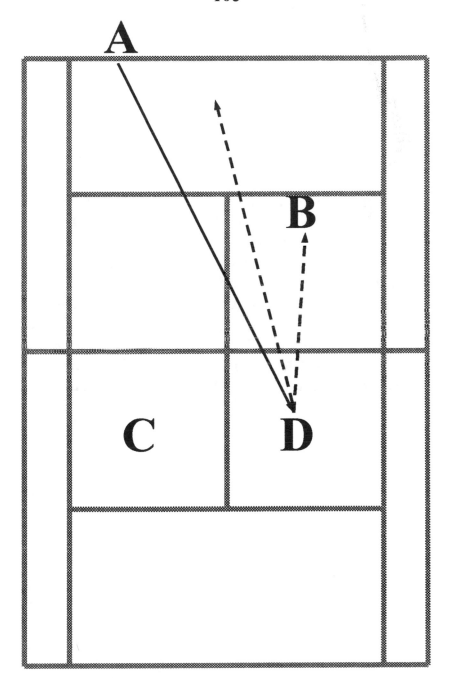

# DRILL # 11. Defense to Offense.

Here the back player works to go from defense to offense.

**A** is back and alternately feeds **C** and **D**, who must first return a nice solid ball (not a killer) to **A** (**11a**). In order to keep **C** and **D** from killing **B** at the net, **A** has three options.

(1) Hit a low shot to **C** or **D**, preferably to the forehand volley (forehand because it is not as natural a shot as the backhand volley).

(2) Hit a hard shot directly at the stomach of **C** or **D**.

(3) Lob over either player's backhand side.

By choosing one of these three alternatives (**11b**), **A** can avoid setting **B** up and go over from defense to offense. Play four balls and rotate. Then as a game, play the first side to 10. If the defensive team wins points with any of these three shots, they receive 2 points instead of 1.

# Drill 11 Defense to Offense (11a)

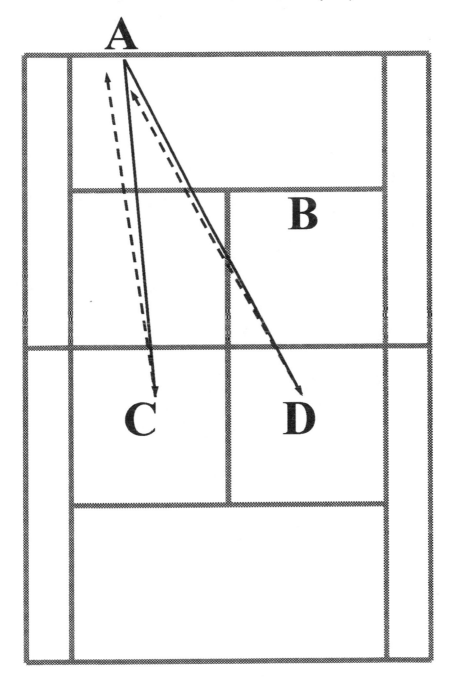

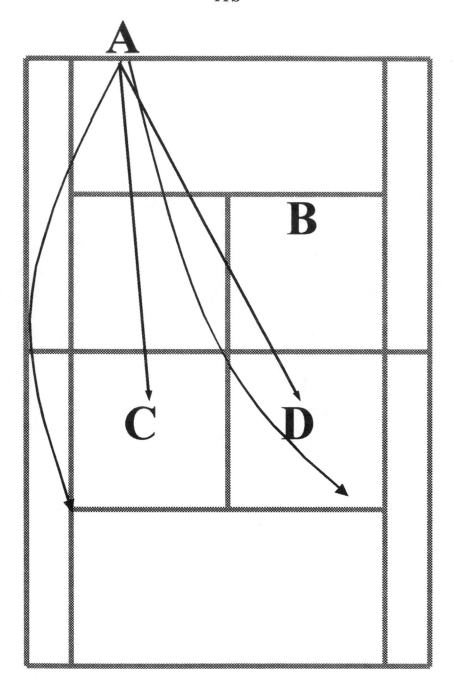

# CHAPTER 4.
# DRILLS FOR INCOMPLETE FOURSOMES

Sometimes, you have that perfect doubles practice match arranged, and either your partner or one or both of your opponents don't show up. Instead of being angry and negative, turn this time into a positive workout session.

For most of these drills, a hopper is recommended. Remember, it doesn't have to be the size that most tennis pros have, but one that is capable of holding about 70 balls. They are available in most sports stores and are relatively inexpensive. This size is more than adequate for all the drills in this book.

# DRILL # 1. Target Hitting (3 players).

Begin with two players (**A** and **B**) at the net with the hopper behind **A**. The third player (**C**) is alone on the opposite side of the net at the regular returning position. The first part of the drill is relatively simple. Player **C** practices target hitting shots alternately at **A** and **B** (**1a**). **A** and **B** are working on depth by hitting volleys deeper than the service line. Occasionally, **A** should feed **C** a short ball, which **C** must return down the center, between **A** and **B** (**1b**). The tendency in real game situations is for players to try to return "sitters" like this down the alley and miss. This drill will encourage hitting between the net players. It will also help the net players work on covering the center as a team. Rotate players every 5 minutes.

# Drill 1 Target Hitting (1a)

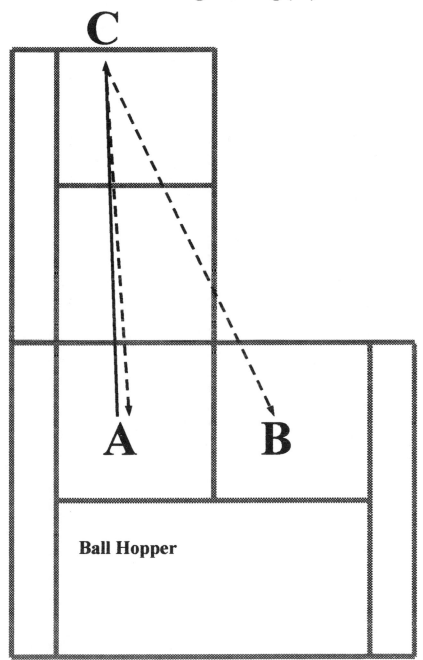

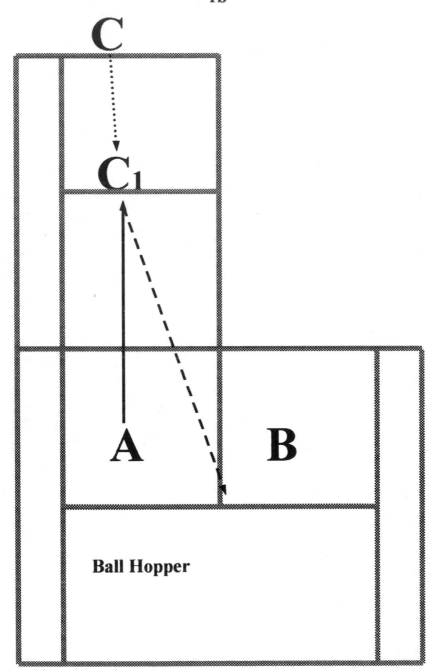

# DRILL # 2. Volleys and Passing Shots
(3 players).

A begins at the net in the deuce court, with **B** and **C** on the opposite side of the net in the back court. (The hopper is behind **B**.) Here, **A** works on hitting deep volleys to **B** and **C**. **B** and **C** try to pass **A** only in the deuce court. Every now and then **B** and **C** should hit lobs to **A**. Rotate position **A** every 5 minutes. Repeat the drill with **A** in the ad court.

# Drill 2 Volleys and Passing Shots

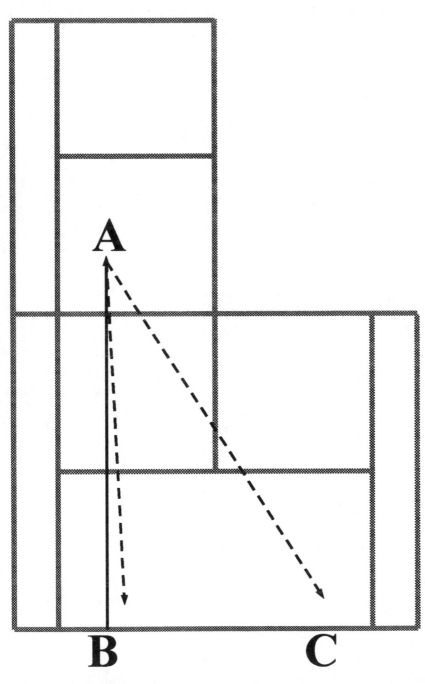

**Ball Hopper**

# DRILL #3. Deep Ground Strokes (3 players).

This drill concentrates on players hitting deep ground strokes. All three players begin on the baseline, with **A** in the deuce court and the hopper behind **B**. **A** should return alternately to **B** and **C** (**3a**). If a ball happens to land short near the service line, players come in to the net to play the point out. For example, if **A** hits short, **B** and **C** move up (**3b**) and vice versa. Rotate positions every 5 minutes. Repeat with **A** in the ad court.

# Drill 3 Deep Ground Strokes (3a)

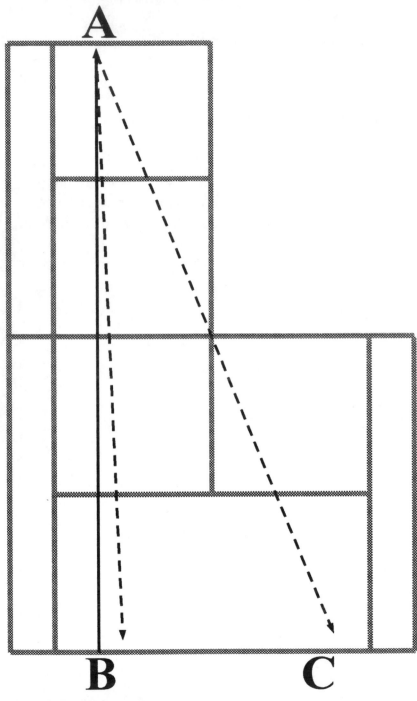

**Ball Hopper**

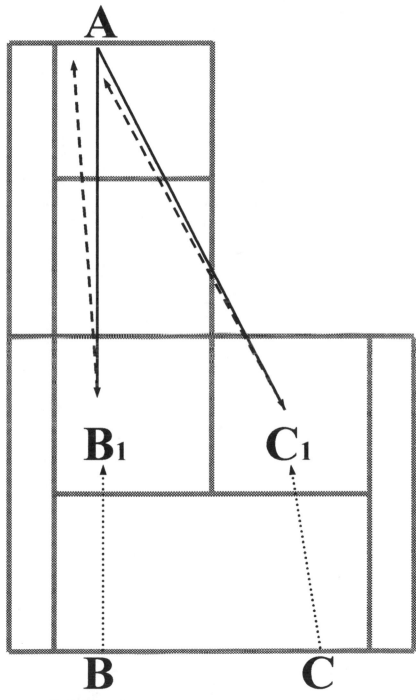

**Ball Hopper**

## DRILL #4. Overheads (3 players).

Begin with **B** and **C** on the baseline (with the hopper behind them). **A** is at the net on the opposite side in the deuce court. **B** and **C** can only hit lobs to **A**, who concentrates on hitting overheads and targeting alternate sides of **B**'s and **C**'s court. If the lob is well behind **A** or unplayable, let it go. The aim of the drill is for **A** to wait on good overhead opportunities. Rotate position **A** every 5 minutes. Repeat with **A** in the ad court.

# Drill 4 Overheads

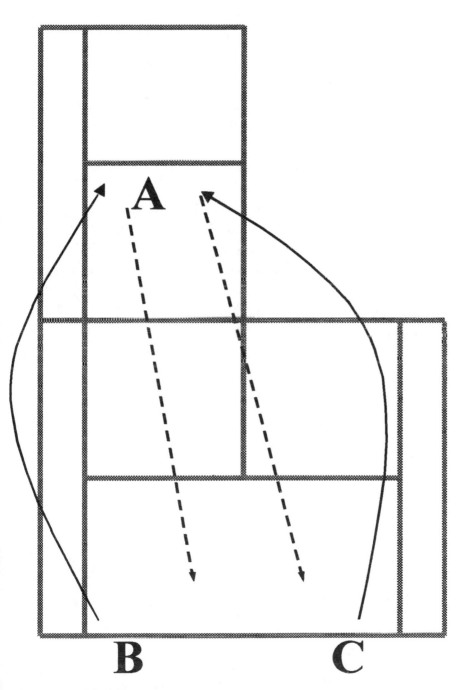

**Ball Hopper**

# DRILL # 5. Playing the Net (3 players).

When you are at the net in doubles, if the ball comes to you below the top of the net, you should volley to your opponent farthest back. If you receive the shot above the net, then hit low at your net opponent. In this drill, you practice both of these scenarios.

Player **A** is back on the baseline in the deuce court with the hopper behind and begins by feeding **C** a volley. If the ball is low below the net, player **C** hits back to **A** (**5a**) and plays the point out. If **A** hits a high ball, **C** nails **B** at the net (**5b**). Continue and rotate positions every 5 minutes. Repeat with **A** in the ad court.

**Ball Hopper**

**Drill 5 Playing the Net**
**5a**

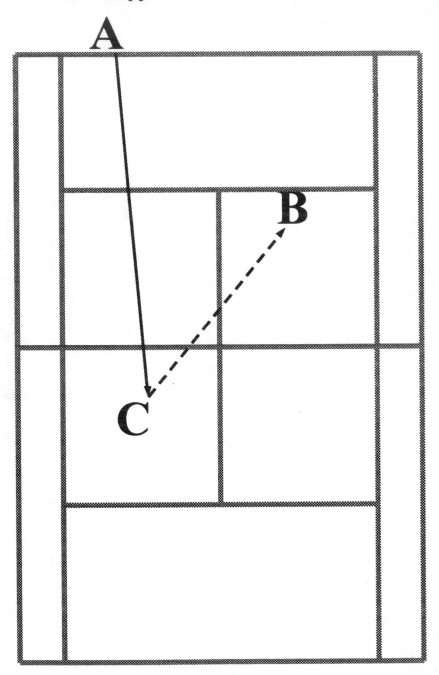

**5b**

# DRILL # 6. Practicing in the Alleys
(2 players).

When there are only 2 players, you usually practice hitting crosscourt to each other, down the line, and one-up, one-back drills. A nice variation to get a better feel for the court is for both players to stand in the alleys at the baselines. Hit to each other in the alleys only, 5 minutes in each alley (**6a**). Then come to the net in the alleys, and hit volleys for 5 minutes; change alleys, and hit for 5 more minutes (**6b**).

# Drill 6 Practicing in the Alleys (6a)

6b

# DRILL #7. Serving and Volleying (2 players).

Practice your serves to each other as if you were playing doubles. **A** serves and comes in to the net. **B** returns the serve. Play the point out crosscourt. **A** serves ten times from the deuce and ten from the ad court; then **B** does the same thing.

## Drill #7A. Serving and Staying Back (2 players).

**A** serves and stays back. **B** returns and comes in. Play the point out crosscourt. **A** serves 10 times from the deuce court and then the ad court. **B** follows, doing the same thing.

# Drill 7 Serving and Volleying

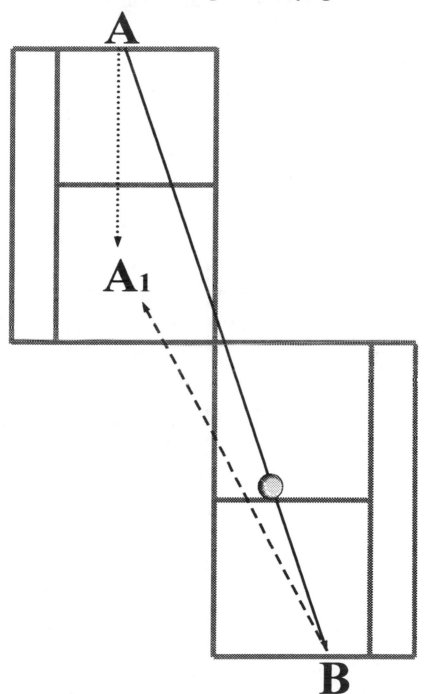

# Drill 7A Serving and Staying Back

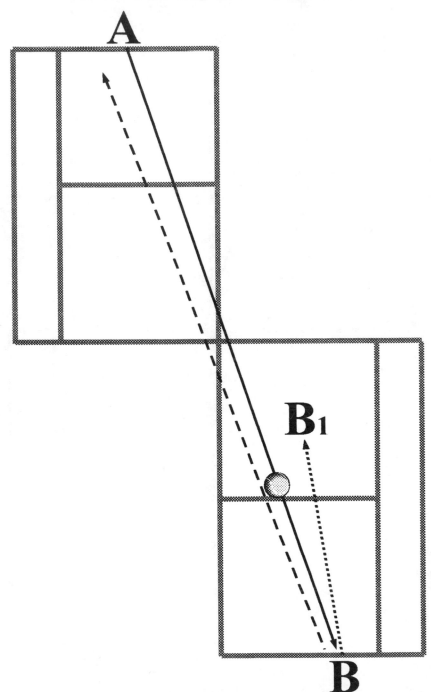

# DRILL # 8. Rally (2 players).

Begin with both players standing at their respective baselines with four balls in their pockets. Each player hits a ball simultaneously, so that the two balls cross the net at roughly the same time. Keep playing the two balls. If you have trouble keeping them in play from the baseline, start closer to the net and gently hit to each other until you get the hang of it. Then move back to the baselines. This drill will help you get set quicker and improve your concentration and eye-hand coordination.

# Drill 8 Rally

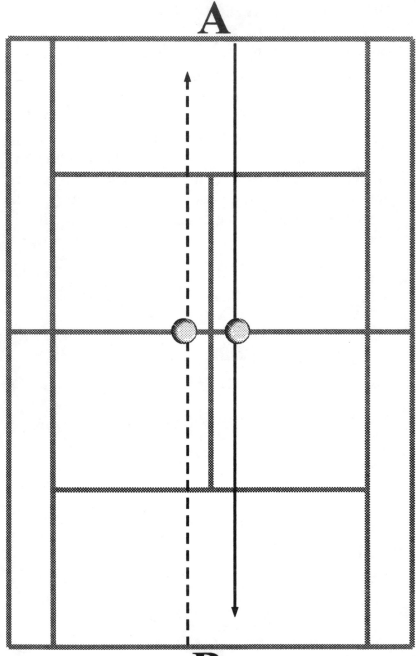

## DRILL # 9. Aiming (1 player).

This drill improves your general feel for the court. Stand close to the net with the hopper next to you. Try to hit 6 shots to the baseline, then 6 shots within one foot of the baseline, then 6 shorter, and shorter, and finally at the service line. While you are doing this, aim your shots for certain positions on the court.

## DRILL # 10. Visualizing the Court (1 player).

Very often players will miss a shot because they are looking where they want to place the ball and not at the ball itself. This drill will help you visualize the court so that you can keep your eye on the ball when you take your shot.

Stand at the net and spend one minute looking at the opposite court. Then close your eyes and try to "see" the court. Practicing this several times will make you feel more comfortable on the court and more aware of the boundaries you have to work with. To confirm your new sight, turn around with your back to the net. First concentrate on looking at the service line. Then close your eyes and try to walk to it. Come back and try in the same way to walk to the baseline and to the alleys with your eyes closed. Repeat three times.

# DRILL # 11. Eye-Hand Coordination
(1 player).

You can do this anywhere to improve your eye-hand coordination. Simply stick your thumb up out in front of you and look at it. Then take your eyes off of it and focus on the background, a wall, fence, or whatever. Look back to your thumb and back to the wall several times. Continue for at least 15 seconds. The point is to improve your focus itself and to shorten the time it takes you to refocus.

# DRILL # 12. Avoiding Hitting Balls That Are Out (2 players).

When we are at the net, in the middle of the court, or in "no man's land," one problem we all have is deciding whether a ball coming to us is going to be out. Here is a drill that will help improve your perception and avoid hitting balls that are going to be out.

From the baseline **B** hits the ball past **A** at the net. **A** lets it go. Without turning around, **A** has to tell **B** whether the ball was in or out and by how much. **B** tells **A** what really happened. **B** continues hitting a variety of shots, including lobs and balls to the sides. **A** has to judge these in the same way. Use up one hopper of balls; switch roles and repeat.

# CHAPTER 5.
# THE MENTAL GAME OF TENNIS

Handling pressure and not choking are essential to successful tennis. We all have days where we will lose matches simply because we will not be strong enough to get through the bad points. The key is to develop a mental attitude that can be carried through and survive these lapses in concentration. The better tennis players will win matches not only when they play well, but also when they are having an off day. Good players find a way to win.

Improving your mental attitude will take time, discipline, and commitment. You will have to work on yourself, on your attitude towards your partner, and the way you look at your opposition.

## YOU

Begin working on yourself first. Being positive on the court is a must. Having a great attitude will not only improve your game and the way you feel about yourself, but will also help you to focus better. Smart players know their capabilities but they are also respectful of their opponents. On the other hand, good players will not let their opponents intimidate them or be distracted by them. Letting the opposition get into your head is one of the quickest ways to lose matches. Successful players will ignore the distraction and will focus throughout the match, regardless of the opposition's tactics. The next two drills will help you improve your mental strength.

## Drill # 1. Concentration.

Take a portable radio with you to practice. For 5 minutes during your workout, turn the radio on full blast. Preferably listen to a type of music that you dislike the most. During those 5 minutes, try to play through the music. In other words, divert your focus from the music to your strokes. After a while, you shouldn't even hear the music, allowing you to fully concentrate on your tennis. At first it may be difficult, but after practicing a few times you should be able to block out the annoying music. This is a great exercise because you will learn to tune out your opponents' habits in just the same way.

## Drill # 2. Mental Toughness.

To improve your (and your partner's) mental toughness put yourself in adverse situations as often as you can for short periods of time. For instance, if you don't like playing in the morning, get up and push yourself to do it. If the sun bothers you, play in the middle of the day. If you like a fast-paced game with hard-hitting shots, arrange    matches against some slow, soft-hitters. By putting yourself in these unwanted situations, you develop focus and confidence. You will learn that once you set your mind to it, you can accomplish anything.

## YOU AND YOUR PARTNER

Now that you've worked on yourself, start working on your attitude towards your partner. First of all, always be supportive and positive about your partners, even when they may not be playing particularly well. Compliment your partner whenever possible. The worst thing you can do for your partner's confidence is to give lectures about what is going wrong. A suggestion once or twice on changing something in the course of a match is fine, but constant advice on strokes and strategy will only make things worse. The good teams are the ones that can figure out a way to win even when they are playing badly. This is achieved by being patient, helpful, and committed to playing with each other.

Successful teams will also identify their opponents' mistakes as quickly as possible. It is equally important to take notice of their strengths. The key is to use that knowledge to your advantage. Respect their great shots, but don't dwell on them. For example, if you start fearing your opponents' big forehands, after a while it will seem even bigger. Simply pay attention to it, but concentrate more on attacking their weaknesses. However, if you stop hitting to their good sides all the time, chances are they will get in a groove, and you don't want that either. So, it is crucial now and then to hit to their strong side and save hitting exclusively to their weaker side for important points. When you are in trouble in a match situation, not only hit to the weaker opponent, but hit to that player's weaker side.

Good teams never change a winning strategy. That is reserved strictly for teams that are losing. If you are winning, stick with whatever it is you're doing!

## SIZING UP YOUR OPPONENTS DURING WARM-UP

Use the time warming up with your opponents before the match to scout their strengths and weaknesses. Here are some suggestions.

**Groundstrokes.** While rallying from the baseline, every now and again hit the ball right at your opponent. A ball that crowds will generally be taken with the best shot. However, some players are better than others at disguising their weaknesses. So, to be really sure whether the forehand or backhand is better, hit a short approach shot right at the body; chances are your opponent will hit it from the best side.

**Volleys.** You and your partner should also pay attention to the velocity of the ball on the volley. If your opponents step in and hit hard, chances are they feel comfortable and like to be at the net. The same is true if they are aggressive, alert, and move their feet. If they seem passive, meek and not particularly powerful, they probably prefer the baseline.

Also, bad volleyers will swing at the low volley just as hard as they do on the high volley. Good volleyers will hit solid high volleys and know how to adjust by taking some pace off on the low ones. They will shorten their swing and stay down longer to keep the ball from popping up. So, throw your opponents a low volley. If they swing at it or pop it up, they are not comfortable at the net. In the match, capitalize on this weakness.

**Serve.** Good servers usually take a lot more warm-up serves than average players. They will pay more attention to getting their serve ready for the match. If your opponents spend a lot of time on their serves, watch out!

**Overheads.** Same idea as the serve.

**Movement.** If by now you have a general idea whether your opponent is a baseline or a net player, always remember that the baseliners usually run better side to side, and volleyers up and back. You might consider tossing the baseliner a short shot, just to see what happens. On the same principle use deep shots and keep the volleyer stretched out on the baseline.

**General Appearance.** Pay attention to your opponents' physiques. How big are they? If one is short and the other tall, make a mental note to hit more lobs over the short one's head and crowd the ball to the other. Generally speaking, taller players don't seem to like the balls hit right at them and low, while the shorter players don't like the balls high and wide. If your opponents are the same height, watch to see which one seems to be more solid and in charge, because this is the player you don't want to hit to on an important point.

Also pay attention to your opponents' body language. The good volleyers will look more confident at the net. They will tend to move their feet more, seem more lively at the net, and will probably warm up the volley longer. The same is true for the baseliners. They will appear more confident and comfortable there.

At the end of the warm up, share your scouting tips with your partner and vice versa. At first this process will seem hard, but after a few weeks of scouting your opposition during warm-up, it will become second nature. You will put yourself in a winning position before the match begins.

# MOMENTUM

Have you ever been in this situation: you're up 5-2, everything is going smoothly, and then before you realize it, nothing is working and you lose? You can't figure out what happened. You probably lost your momentum and couldn't get it back quickly enough to recover. By playing smart, you can increase your chances of maintaining your momentum or changing it back in your favor.

In that 5-2 lead, you may have had a very quick following game, losing three straight points, getting into a hole at love-40, and then losing the game. This is where the momentum begins to change in your opponents' favor. They will capitalize on it, and you find yourself losing several games in a row. Tennis needs to be treated like basketball at times; take a time out when down. So instead of rushing to the next point, take your full 25 seconds between points. Talk to your partner, play with your strings, tie your shoe laces, etc. Use your time in between points to slow down your opponents' momentum. Conversely, when things are going well for you, keep the pace of the match going to help maintain your positive momentum.

Remember that the most important games in a match are the odd ones: 3, 5, 7, 9, etc. These games determine the direction of the set, whether one team will gain a bigger lead, or whether the gap will close.

For instance, after these crucial games, the score will be either 2-1 or 3-0; 3-2 or 4-1; 4-3 or 5-2, etc. So play with the knowledge that these games are important and heighten your awareness of smart shots. And, don't forget about the first two points in each game, because by winning these you put extra pressure on the opposition.

# DRILL # 1. Maintaining Momentum.

**A** and **B** play **C** and **D** as though the score is love-40 in **C** and **D**'s favor. **C** and **D** are on the verge of gaining the momentum away from **A** and **B**. What **A** and **B** need to do is to prolong the point as long as possible, keeping the ball in play with high percentage shots. The same applies to 15-40. Play four love-40 points with **A** serving and then four with **B** serving. Then do four 15-40 points with each serving. Reverse roles with **C** and **D** down love-40 and 15-40, and repeat the drill.


# DRILL # 2. Seizing Momentum.

Here **A** and **B** serve 4 points each at 40-love and 40-15. In this situation, try to deliver a knock-out. Be more aggressive. Take some chances. Go for that quick winner down the line, etc. Switch with **C** and **D** serving.

## DRILL # 3. Shifting the Balance.

If your team is receiving at 30-30, be more aggressive. This is the time to shift the balance to your side. For example, after your return, go to the net and try to isolate your opponents' net player on your next shot. If you are serving at 30-30, hit high percentage shots; don't try anything fancy. **A** and **B** serve 4 balls and switch with **C** and **D** serving 4 balls at 30-30.

## DRILL # 4. At the Brink.

If your team is serving at 40-30, play a little more aggressively, but make sure you play solid doubles. When you are down 30-40, play as if you had just one serve. Often your opponents gain confidence by seeing your second serve, and they will cream it. When you are at the break point, play as if you had just one serve and keep everything in the singles court. **A** and **B** try that with 4 points each; then reverse roles with **C** and **D** serving 4 points at 30-40.

## DRILL # 5. Not Losing It.

When you are serving at love-30, you have to be careful because the momentum is starting to shift. Play solid points with high percentage shots. Concentrate on not losing it. **A** and **B** serve 4 balls each at love-30. Switch with **C** and **D** serving 4 each. If you are receiving at love-30, be aggressive and put all the pressure you can on your opponents; i.e., play as if you had nothing to lose. You can afford to gamble. **A** and **B** serve 4 balls each to **C** and **D** at 30-love. Switch roles with **C** and **D** serving.

# DRILL # 6. Maintaining Concentration
(2 players).

If the ball keeps getting hit to your partner and you are not directly involved in a point, it is easy to relax and become a spectator and not a player. Then you may not be ready when the ball does come to you. Try this drill to help you get in the habit of being ready and always "in the point" every time.

With you at the baseline and your partner at the net on the opposite side, have your partner feed you shots to return. But you should start by letting every other ball go by without hitting it, even if you have to move out of the way. Do this for 2 minutes. Then for the next 3 minutes have your partner call whether the shot should be returned or not as it is fed to you. Repeat the drill with you feeding your partner at the baseline.

Tennis is a point-by-point tactical battle. Practicing these situations can significantly help your team. You and your partner will get in the habit of responding with the correct tactical mind-set to the same situations in real matches. Mental preparation almost always precedes success.

# MENTAL PREPARATION

Here are some tips that will help you prepare mentally.

## Music.

Try listening for a few minutes before your match to the kind of music that affects you emotionally. If you are a very mellow person, listen to something that gets you stirred up. If you are nervous before matches, listen to something that will calm you down. Try different kinds of music to see what gets you into the emotional and mental mode that's right for you. This can make a difference in your concentration and quality of play.

## Vizualizing Good Shots.

Watch good players make good shots, in real life or on T.V. Store up in your mind pictures of them doing these shots. Then, when you get on the court, recall the pictures and imagine yourself executing your shots, as you make them, in exactly the same way, confidently and successfully. Similarly avoid watching bad players hit shots. That will build up the wrong kind of pictures in your mind.

**Imaging.**

When you find yourself in tough situations and you know that you are in trouble in the match, you need to dig down inside to pull yourself together. A good way to do this is positive self-imaging. Don't try to use it all the time, but only on the most crucial points. Here's how. Have your partner feed you about 60 balls or use the ball machine. Practice your favorite or most reliable shot. After every good shot, touch your opposite hand. Do this consistently for twelve sessions on the court, but continue to do it off the court as well. Every time you touch your hand, imagine hitting that perfect shot. At first it will be hard to implement, but with time it will become more natural.

Then for two weeks, try this during play. For example, when you are down love-40, touch your hand, and imagine hitting that perfect shot before the point begins. The key here is that it will work for any shot, not just that favorite one you practiced with. This mental focus will improve your overall confidence for that point and help you to feel more secure and alert. So you can hit crosscourt or whatever, but with a positive attitude.

**Pre-Match Jitters.**

If you get nervous or uptight before a match or before a point, physical activity will help you get over it. If you tend to freeze up and can't move your feet, jump rope for a few minutes before your match. And always move and jump before receiving a serve (watch how active the pros are on T.V., preparing themselves to receive the serve).

If you have a medium or long swing, practice hitting the ball more quickly with your partner for five minutes before the match. With both of you on the baseline, concentrate on increasing the speed of your racquet head, swinging faster than usual. Aim your shots about a yard behind the service line. This will help you get physically and mentally up for the match.

If you have a shorter, more compact stroke, practice for five minutes before the match with your partner at the net and you at the opposite baseline. Target hit shots straight at your partner's body as hard as you can. This will relieve any anxiety and get you physically and mentally ready for the match.

**After-the-Match Thoughts.**

If you walk away a winner, enjoy the moment. Reflect on your match and talk about the good and the bad points of your game. Enjoy the positive experience, but be objective.

If you lose, don't dwell on it after the match. You will end up dragging yourself down more than you should. Wait until the next day after you have cooled off, and then review what you did wrong, but in a positive way, so that you develop a game plan to improve.

# CHAPTER 6.
# PHYSICAL FITNESS AND CONDITIONING

Many of you do not have time for conditioning, and, of course, working out for extended periods of time can be quite boring. Running, aerobics, stretching, etc., can take the fun out of the game. The following workouts, each designed to take 5 minutes or less, will help your conditioning while working on your game at the same time. They are all tennis related and are strictly designed to help you become faster and stronger in tennis. Any one of them can be done on a daily basis.

You may extend all the drills described. The great thing is that you can pick and choose which exercises you like to do. You do not have to do them all. Ideally, stretching exercises are always desirable, but for those of you who hate to do them, there is nothing better than swimming to stretch and build up your muscles. Just don't do it right before you play tennis! You'd be surprised what a physical workout that can be.

# DRILL # 1. Reach and Reaction.

The purpose of this drill is to help your poaching skills by stretching your reach and improving your reaction time.

Begin by standing in the ready position with racquet in hand. While bending at the waist, cross over with your left foot and stretch to touch the ground to your right with your racquet. Make sure that you are stepping in a slightly forward crossing motion, so as to simulate catching the ball out in front. Immediately return to the ready position and cross with your right leg while reaching to touch your racquet as far to the left as possible. Do this for 30 seconds as fast as you can. Two sets of 30 seconds would be ideal. If you master that, then try to increase to three sets.

# DRILL # 2. The Triangle.

There is always a tendency to hesitate or move to the side before running forward. Here you work on eliminating any hesitation or side motion and taking the quickest and most direct path to the ball. Think of the net as the base of a triangle, and you are completing the other two sides of the triangle moving diagonally to the net.

Stand on the "T" of the service courts. Run to the point where the alley line meets the net on the deuce side. Touch the net with your racquet. Run backwards to the starting point. Immediately run to the opposite side where the alley line meets the net. Then run backwards to the "T". Do this as fast as you can six times for one set. Take a break and try another set.

# DRILL # 3. Covering the Court Up and Back.

Work on moving quickly. Start at the service line and sprint to the net; touch it with your racquet and run back. As you near the service line, jump with both feet off the ground and pretend to hit an overhead. When you finish, you should be slightly behind the service line. Sprint to the net again and repeat six times at first, for one set. Then work up to two sets.

# DRILL # 4. Moving Properly on the Baseline.

Begin in the center of the baseline in the ready position. Using side-steps, move to your right towards the alley. In the alley, stop, pretend to hit a forehand, and recover to the ready position. Then push off with your outside (right) leg to gain momentum and return to the center where you started, using the same side-steps. Repeat the drill to your left and pretend to hit a backhand in the left alley. Push off with your left leg and return to the center of the baseline. Continue as fast as you can through six forehands and six backhands for one set. Do four sets, and work up to six.

# DRILL # 5. Changing Direction.

In order to move quickly and effectively with your doubles partner you must always be ready to switch directions while you are moving.

Stand facing your partner. The object is to shadow you partner's movements. Choose one of you to be the leader for the first 30 seconds. Move sideways on the balls of your feet, not flat-footed, with the leader switching directions at random. Your partner must mimic your movements and changes in directions. After 30 seconds, take a short break and the follower now becomes the leader for an additional 30 seconds. Repeat the process.

## DRILL # 6. Interval Training for Overall Tennis Shape.

Jog slowly for 30 seconds, then increase to a medium pace for the next 15 seconds. Without stopping, run as fast as you can for 15 more seconds. Then walk for one minute. Repeat for a total of four minutes. As you build up stamina, you can increase the times. For example, increase your run time to 45, 30, and 30 seconds, and your walk time to one minute, 45 seconds. The key is to balance the walking and running, so that you walk for as long as the total combination of the run.

## DRILL # 7. Reach at the Net. (You'll need balls and your partner.)

Begin at the net in the center of the court. Move with small steps first to the right and then to the left. While you are moving, have your partner feed you slow, fairly high volleys from the center baseline. You should aggressively kill these. Try this with 20 balls. Trade places, and you feed your partner 20 balls. Each of you do three sets.

**DRILL  # 8.  Bow-Tie Drill.** (Balls and your partner are required.)

This works on increasing your speed and quickness as you cross over in doubles, and helps your overall performance at the net with volleys and overheads.

Start at the middle of the service court on the deuce side. Have your partner at the opposite baseline feed you a deep overhead so that you are pushed back to return it. Your partner should then feed you a volley to the ad side, bringing you in diagonally across to the ad court. That should be followed by a deep overhead to the ad side moving you back, and finally a volley to the deuce side, bringing you diagonally in to where you started. Repeat five times.